Chrysalis

By Anna K. Abbi

Anna K. Abbi is a retired business professional who splits her time between California and southern Vermont. In retirement, she enjoys working on her books, creating stained glass art, and spending time with her two Rhodesian Ridgeback dogs and her 50-year-old parrot. She writes memoir and fiction under a pen name.

This book is dedicated to those who never give up. I am not suggesting we can live forever—just that we should live ferociously until the end.

Chapter 1

*O*pen *your eyes*, I thought.

I felt the warm night touch my cheek. A breeze. Dust. Whiff of exhaust. Someone took my hand. "You're okay," said a male voice I didn't recognize, piercing the quiet.

"I can't see you. What happened?"

"Car accident. You're on the street—I'll stay with you."

"Thank you."

His voice was sweet; reassuring.

"Can you sing?" I asked him.

I heard the smile in his tone. "I can try." Humming—Silent Night.

He smelled of my Uncle Frank's Old Spice aftershave; comforting. I held his hand in a strong grip. He stayed right there, just as he said he would. We were two strangers lying at the edge of a highway, singing Christmas songs in July. I think it kept me alive. I was not alone.

"Don't leave me." I felt his hand shake. *Am I dying?* His answer was a sob.

The BUZZ in my head took over. "The ambulance is here. They'll help you now." He touched my cheek. "Good luck. I'll pray for you."

"Okay," I said, dropping his hand. There was a loud BUZZ again. The sound of sirens. I looked at the blurred ceiling of the ambulance, then things went black once more. Someone was screaming. Was it me? *Mauricio! Mauricio!* Suddenly, a white ceiling and white curtain formed a small treatment room around me. I struggled to see my surroundings.

"You're in the Pomona Valley Hospital emergency room." A woman's voice. "We can help you and your friend. You've been in a car accident. Try not to call out—hold still if you can."

Mauricio was behind a curtain next to me saying, "Shut up, Anna, I'm here." The side of my head ached.

A doctor was explaining, "I am reattaching your

ear." Out again. Screaming again. *Mauricio!*

"Shut up, damn it!"

Again that BUZZ. I was in the hospital hall along the wall, alone, frightened. I struggled to stay awake. Lost.

"We're sending you home," someone said. "Your ride is here. Get up."

They pulled me by my arms from a horizontal position to sitting. I scooted to stay flat. I was in excruciating pain, my body on fire. Screaming again and again. Glenna, my ride, yelled, "Stop! Something is wrong!" I heard her but couldn't respond. I felt a vague sense of relief that she was there.

"We'll just take her to your car." A man's voice. "We can wrap her in this blanket."

"No! She won't even take aspirin! I won't take her out of the ER. NO!" Glenna was crying. "Something is very wrong."

Back to the hallway. BUZZ in my head again, awake again. They flopped me into a hospital bed, decided to use a backboard, then flopped me back on a gurney—back into bed. Screaming with each flop. Unable to defend myself.

"She is so dramatic," some woman commented.

"Yeah, they tried to release her from the ER, but they had to keep her because of all the screaming," someone else replied.

BUZZ.

The green hospital walls dimmed and disappeared.

"Are you awake? I'm your day nurse, Lynna. It's 7:30 a.m."

I tried to open my eyes.

The woman looked about 35. She was muscular, fit, and tan, wearing a crisp white uniform and the words RN on her badge. Her dark brown hair was pulled back into a ponytail, and her eyes, which were the same color, were smiling. For some reason, I liked her, even in my stupor. Her movement and attitude were positive and reassuring.

I heard her but couldn't answer from my deep, silent place. It was the most comfortable I had ever felt—soft, warm, unafraid.

"Do you know what day it is?" She leaned in to be heard better, using a slower, more pronounced tone. I had no desire to respond.

BUZZ. I realized her presence, but then there was nothing. It was like being in a floating room with no floor, ceiling, or walls.

Blurred and confused, awake... The fluorescent

lights sped by on the ceiling. A bang through swinging doors, a loud thump. I realized I was in the hall again, being moved. There was a person at my head pushing the gurney. He looked down at me and smiled.

"Where am I?" I asked.

"Hello, I'm Julian. We're taking a cervical x-ray—is that okay?"

Do I get to vote? I wondered, feeling jarred. "What x-ray?"

"For your neck," he offered.

"Why? Is something wrong?"

"Just put her in the hall," someone ordered. "We have a few ahead of her."

"Got it," Julian replied. "Don't forget her."

I was awake, looking at the light green ceiling. I had no recollection of the x-ray. Several men and women in hospital garb collected around me. "What's wrong?" I said, alarmed. They placed heavy sandbags all around my head, my torso, and my legs, as well as on my chest and forehead.

"You have to wait for your doctor," Julian answered. He sadly patted my head.

Now I was alert, breathless with the extra weight on my body. "I can't breathe," I cried. "Did you find something?" No one replied.

It took eight people to carefully roll me back to

my room. No banging through swinging doors; no flopping me back in bed. Out again. Early morning.

Visiting hours were noon to 3 p.m. and 7 to 8 p.m. I could tell people were in my room, but my deep cavern would not allow me to communicate. It was great comfort—quiet, warm, a place so soothing. I did not want to leave. During this day I was not afraid, and though I screamed, I don't think it was due to pain. *This must be how death would feel*, I thought, *very soft and smooth. Nothing to fear.*

As I began to creep out of my cave that afternoon, it was as though the temperature changed suddenly. Voices in the hospital hallway were loud and tense. A hulk of a man turned the corner and entered my room. He was red-faced with anger and his six-foot-plus, bulky frame seemed to fill the room. His dark eyes stuck out of his jowly face.

I was immediately repulsed and afraid. My grandmother would have described him as a man who walked like he had huge balls and a two-inch cock. Good one, Grandma.

"What the hell are all these people doing here?"

As he cast his glance around the room, each

visitor flinched when he passed over them. No one moved or made a sound. When his gaze landed on my three former roommates—I called them my gaggle of gays—he looked them up and down in disgust. I noticed Mauricio, the fourth roommate and the friend riding with me when the accident happened, was missing.

The man was flanked by two nurses, one of which offered, "They're visiting, Dr. McDaniel."

If looks could injure, she would have lost an appendage. Her expression was panicked. It seemed nurses would be accustomed to this bombastic type of man, but she was not. I somehow felt responsible for her discomfort.

"No visitors means no visitors!" he said quietly, baring his very white teeth. "What the hell does a physician need to do? Can't you read?" He spit as he spoke.

The smaller of the two nurses brightened as if she knew the answer, then thought better of it. She cast her eyes toward the floor and folded her arms in defense. McDaniel raised both of his in a defeated gesture. *Now who's dramatic?* I thought. I had actually conjured the strength to feel resistance to this awful man. But it quickly dissipated as I took in his contagious fury.

My mouth was dry. I struggled to speak.

"Can I have a drink?" The smaller nurse held a cup of water with a straw for me. I managed a big slurp.

When I was a young girl, my grandma would put googly eyes on a peanut and tuck it into a stick matchbox bed with a colorful square of flannel. That's exactly how I felt tucked under a blanket in that hospital bed—googly-eyed, breathless, and very confused. As I looked around the room, every face was stunned.

I had managed—reluctantly—to come out of my quiet place into the bright hospital room. Then Dr. McDaniel cast his wrath toward me. I stayed in my matchbox and met his eyes as best I could, a bit calmer now. I noticed that the badge on his coat read "neurosurgeon."

"And you," McDaniel said to me. It was my turn. "What are you thinking?" A flurry of potential answers flew through my tattered mind, including *Nothing*, *You're an ass!*, and *What the hell are you screaming about?*

"Why? What's wrong?" I was losing my composure, tears streaming down my cheeks, hoping he would slow down. I've always hated that I cry in response to a bully. It does work, sometimes. But not this time.

"You have a broken neck."

When he spoke the words, they echoed in my head like someone had dropped a metal bedpan. Stunned, I struggled to comprehend, but I could not.

"No, I do not," I insisted.

All the air left that room. I couldn't breathe; one of the nurses placed an oxygen mask on my face. "Should I call for a trach, Doctor?"

"No," he answered, "let her recover. She thinks she knows better than me." He snorted.

No one in the room had taken the doctor's advice to leave, so a collective howl went up and into the hall. Billy, the tallest and most effeminate of my friends, fainted. "Oh, for Christ's sake!" McDaniel screamed. "Get that faggot out of here!" The two nurses unceremoniously dragged Billy into the hall, his purse still clutched in his hand.

My most athletic friend, Robin, turned toward the doc with fire in his eyes. "No, Robin, don't touch him!" cried Kip. They gathered themselves and retreated to the hall, still weeping loudly.

It must have been the stress, but Glenna started to laugh uncontrollably. One of the nurses joined in, and soon we all descended into nervous, frantic giggles—except our infuriated neurosurgeon.

At least it broke his cadence. *Why would such an ass want to be a doctor?* I thought. *Well, duh. The money.* The loss of control angered him so much that I half thought he could explode or drop dead right there.

By now, almost all the medical staff on duty were in the hallway, along with pretty much every ambulatory patient. Some of the staff were trying to attend to Billy, and some were trying to get a glimpse into the action going on in my room.

"Jesus. No one told you." All at once, McDaniel seemed to comprehend the situation. For a moment, he just stood in the middle of the room, looking at his shoes. He was finally quiet, though it was unclear whether he was taking stock of his mistake or planning his next attack.

I was still conscious, but the googly-eye effect was intensifying. Now my friends that had come to cheer me were all in the hall in tears, and they were not the silent style but the boohoo variety. He again roared they must go, get out of the hospital, and so they left, skittering away like gay little mice. My girlfriend, Glenna, stayed and walked to my bedside, as did the nurses. I finally asked, "What do we do about it?" Somehow I felt, for that moment, encouraged to have a diagnosis. But what now?

My eyes searched each face as they arranged themselves around my bed. No answer presented itself. I looked for my friendly BUZZ. But it did not take me away this time. I had to stay present, despite the pounding in my head and the darkening cloud of anxiety gathering around me.

McDaniel looked right at me with no compassion.

"You're a quad—a quadriplegic. You will never leave that bed." He smirked as if he had won the game.

He stood up and adjusted his belt in what seemed a prideful gesture. *You son of a bitch*, I thought. Then, he actually farted—loudly! Shocked, I frantically turned my eyes to the faces around my bed. No one reacted.

What kind of pig is this guy? One moment he says your life is over, the next he's relieving his gas pain, I thought. *My God!*

We all looked as repulsed as was safe. The doctor seemed amused. His laugh was tense, awkward—like it wasn't used much.

Glenna said, "I can take care of her." McDaniel walked toward her, and she began to back away. He sort of chuckled, almost seeming delighted. He towered over her small frame. At only 110 pounds and five foot two, she had always reminded me of a pretty porcelain doll. She did her best to glare at him with those soft brown eyes. He chuckled again.

"How old are you?" he boomed. She tearfully

replied that she was 21, looking like she might faint. "You can't do that and won't want to in a few months. I'm a neurosurgeon, one of the best. Her spinal cord is gone. You can't cure that."

Maybe you can't, I thought. *So who can?*

He looked back to me. "You will not improve," he said coldly. "The sooner you accept that, the better."

Why would anyone accept that option?

I searched his face for the joke. I had tickets to Europe on the 18th, had just completed my master's degree, and was ready to seek my first job as a clinical counselor. Glenna and I lived across from the ocean in Newport Beach—my first live-in relationship. I had important plans for my life that were already in motion.

I'd already picked out my office, and I'd worked hard to have enough money to last me until my client base was built out. The vacation to Europe was already planned and paid for. In a moment of denial I wondered, *Could I delay the trip?* I didn't know it then, but there was no way I'd be getting on that plane.

I felt I was engulfed in a bad dream but couldn't wake up. At that point, I think I was too shocked to panic. That would come later. For now, all I could do was resist. Was it all lost? No! It couldn't be over! There was no way this accident, this asshole doctor would take it all away from me.

I couldn't breathe. A nurse again lovingly hooked me up to the oxygen mask and cast her eye at McDaniel; he shook his head no. Everyone was silent, and anger rose up inside me—not the tearful type, but the killer type. I tried to consider the possible consequences of my knee-jerk instinct, but it seemed to be my only course of action.

I signaled to the nurse with my eyes to remove the mask and, with every bit of intention, looked at this mean bull of a doctor.

"You are a total son of a bitch. How can you be this destructive with your patients?"

Gradually, his eyes widened.

"You're fired," I slowly articulated with deliberate disdain. I shook so hard that the bed rattled, to my embarrassment. I even wet myself, though I guess it could have been worse. Glenna, looking startled, put her hand on my forehead. She was agreeing with my decision.

Surprised, McDaniel laughed that strange laugh. He looked at me with a slight hint of respect, but it was gone in a fraction of a second. "Order a psychiatric evaluation for this woman," he snarled at the closest nurse. "Clearly, she's fucking nuts."

"If you don't want to help me, you can't be my doctor. Don't you ever touch me or order a procedure for me. You. Are. Fired," I said weakly, and began gratefully receding back into my sweet cave.

As I lost consciousness, a nurse said, "He's the only neuro doctor in Pomona."

But I was already back in my matchbox.

Chapter 2

"Good morning! Do you remember me?" Lynna, the day nurse, greeted me. I tried to respond, but no voice came. "Do you know you're at Pomona Valley Hospital?" She seemed so upbeat about everything, somehow; it lifted me up. "What do you remember?"

Flashes of the accident started to come back to me. The gorgeous purplish hue of a summer's night in Pomona. Mauricio, asleep in the passenger seat. The blurry image of a car hurtling toward us as I made a legal left turn. The sound of shattering glass. The smell of asphalt, oppressive against my face.

"Is... Is Mauricio dead? Did he die in the crash?"

Lynna furrowed her brow. "I'm sorry, I don't know anything about your friend. He wasn't my patient."

Gulping, I swallowed down the rest of my questions. The way she used the past tense made me feel almost certain he had to be dead. Why else wouldn't he be here?

I stared back at her. "I think I was told I was paralyzed. And I fired my doctor." I was as tired as I have ever felt. If my head fell to one side, I just left it there.

She took note of my despondent demeanor but just kept bouncing around my room. "So many people sent you flowers." She held them toward me so I could take in the scent.

"Thanks." Perhaps for the first time since this ordeal had started, I smiled.

She beamed. "You are the *hit* of the hospital." She giggled. "No one likes that bastard McDaniel! Your ortho doctor, Dr. Sailor, asked a neuro guy, Dr. Waters, to take your case. He said yes. He's from Riverside. So you don't need to worry about that." She paused. "You're the first broken neck at PVH."

"Is that a good thing?" I asked.

"Just a thing."

"Do I get a say in who will be my doctor?"

"Don't look a gift horse in the mouth," she answered. "He's a favorite of Dr. Sailor's—comes highly recommended. He may also be the only one willing to travel."

I was too tired to care.

"Okay," I slowly answered, trying to stay present. From that day on, I never questioned what Lynna told me. I held a great deal of respect and trust for nursing, back then and now still—they're there every moment. If you make it, it's because of your nurses. They are vastly underappreciated.

"He'll be here soon to check up on you. Also, you've had a string of visitors and calls." She bounded out of the room.

I was still struggling to stay lucid when that shadow came over the hallway. McDaniel entered the room. He took up all the space and air, relegating me to my tiny matchbox and googly eyes.

"Well, here she is as I told you, Dr. Waters," McDaniel said loudly. "My only failure." He laughed, stopping at the doorway. "She cried and carried on last visit, so I don't think she'll be any more trouble. We also had to fend off a coven of queer visitors, though I see that is not a problem today." He sneered.

Hate is not an emotion I often find in me, but I was willing to make an exception for him. I'd never recommend it, though—hate only breeds sadness and sickness.

The last thing I heard from McDaniel was another

very loud fart. No one reacted to his exit. The lack of decorum seemed consistent with his personality.

Dr. Jason Waters got a chair and sat down. He was beautiful—very fit and tan with a shaved head and bright, soft blue eyes. His voice was low and gentle, and he smelled of pine. He was a very soft-spoken human, someone I wouldn't want to disappoint. I hoped he was the bearer of better news.

"You've had a rough start, and this will be a long journey," he said. "To set you on the path to your future, I have to do some procedures. It won't be easy. Within the next few days, I must get the traction away from your jaw. To do that and improve the weight of the pressure on your neck, we'll place two holes in your skull to hold the traction; basically, it will realign your vertebrae. We can use a local anesthetic for that—no feeling in your skull."

He looked me in the eyes as he explained the procedures. *Maybe a chance is possible,* I thought. But I was afraid to ask, so I resolved to wait and see. I realized the odds were not in my favor.

I stared at the ceiling tiles. I must have been pale. *How could this be real?* I thought. *One thing's for sure—it definitely isn't fair.* Defeat was a new sensation for me. My subconscious was kicking in, saying, *Never will*

I stay in this position. How did people face this? How could I?

"Next, we must surgically remove a bone splinter in the top back side of your skull; it's causing pressure on your brain. That's a little more complicated. Then Dr. Sailor will take you to the surgery and put a Minerva cast on. It goes from the top of your head to your waist with your arms, face, and ears open. He's an army battleground surgeon and thinks it might help. They, in my experience, do outstanding work. Innovative ideas—exactly what is needed here." Wait... was that hope I detected in his voice?

Now I really couldn't breathe. Dr. Waters turned the oxygen higher. "You're in shock from what I've explained. I'll stay until you have questions." I tried to get control, to relax. I wanted to cry, sob, complain about how unfair it all was, but all I could do was stare at that damn ceiling tile.

As he took my hand, I realized I couldn't feel his touch. My head was pounding. Panic filled my mind as I tried to think of questions. The problem with questions is that you get answers, and so far, that wasn't working out very well for me.

"What do the tongs look like?" He sort of smiled, looking relieved.

Dr. Waters said, "Like the old tongs for block

ice." Then he realized I knew what that was. We used ice boxes when I was a kid, and those things were huge!

I croaked, my terrified eyes the size of saucers. The urge to get up and walk out of the hospital coursed through me. I couldn't, of course.

"No, no—here, look." He pulled a surgical piece of steel the size of his hand out of his kit. "See," he laughed, "they look like they're from an icehouse for tiny people, but we're better than that in 1963." We both found that funny. Relief washed over me; I had made the right knee-jerk decision. It was the first time I'd felt calm since this began, at least while conscious.

I did, when able and with Glenna's help, look up why some neurosurgeons are such cold people. Believe it or not, it's a known, researched subject. Some of them become hardened to the patients. They might work miracles to keep them alive, but not the way a patient wants to live. Neurosurgery is a difficult specialty, and McDaniel seemed to take the pressure out on his patients. I was disgusted.

A few days later, as I waited to undergo the

procedures that would determine my prognosis, I turned 25, though I really felt a half century old.

My friends came, some holding up, some sad. I kept thinking it was like attending my own happy funeral. By now I felt, in some existential way, that I had died. At least the struggle of my life, happy though it was, was over. I no longer needed to scrape my way through work and school. Whatever happened now would be different.

A couple of my night nurses snuck in a bottle of champagne and a long straw. They gave me two sips to celebrate. We all laughed and enjoyed and got rowdy. It's still one of the best birthdays I've ever had. Supported by the love of friends, I started to believe that maybe my soul could heal, even if my body could not.

The following day, they placed the holes in my head for the tongs. The surgery was a small room, with one doctor—Dr. Waters—and one very frightened nurse in training, Angela. I was awake, wishing I were any other place; it seemed she was of the same frame of mind. Doc instructed her, "Just hold the head to resist the drill." I could feel her shake.

As I lay there waiting for an "Ah!" or an "Oh no" to signal a mistake, the drill sound in my head was as scary as anything so far. At least he did not whistle as he worked. "Okay," he said. "I'm in." I wished he hadn't told me. There was no pain, only fear.

I wished to return to my soft, quiet cocoon, but no. When Nurse Nervous resisted, her hand was under my chin—she was choking me. The doctor thought I was crying and tried to get the job done. For the first time, I realized I couldn't move to help myself. The bells started going off on the heart monitor. He looked at what she was doing and grabbed her hand away. Safe again!

She left the room wailing loudly. He apologized several times, but he never blamed Angela—commendable, I thought. "I should have given her more instruction," he said. "I promise I will next time."

Next time? I wondered. *Oh God, I'm not going to survive this.* Fear landed within me like an anchor as I once again realized how injured I was, and how easy it would be to succumb to a small mistake. After all, mistakes happen every day.

My first hospital stay was not like the doctor shows on TV; it was much more haphazard. This really was like a floppy, disorganized battleground. And as you go along, you realize that's just what you can detect—close calls happen all the time that you don't even notice. If I could stay alive, it was going to be up to me. Every small thing was so important that it could be a life-and-death result. And that was with all the people involved doing their very best, with very few exceptions.

Then the tongs were in. I came out of the room on something called a Stryker burn-frame bed. I must have passed out because I woke up in my room. The bed was like a bicycle seat for your whole body—a seat for my head, one for my middle, and one for my shoulders. The idea was if the patient's skin was burned, the bed didn't touch their body much. But I was not burned—was I?

There was a large bolt at the top to turn the burned patient over after being sandwiched between the flat top and bottom apparatus. My traction was fixed to the bed and to my head. If that bolt was accidentally yanked, it was goodbye. They told me, "Don't ever let anyone pull this bolt." *And how would I stop them?* I thought wryly.

I dutifully informed every person who approached. "Oh, this bolt?" some people would say in jest, as if they were about to yank it clean out. Very funny! I had always been somewhat touchy about my safety; this put me over the edge.

I was lost as to what time it was. After I peed on the floor, they realized I wasn't positioned correctly; the pee place was under my shoulders.

Three concerned nurses pulled my body up to place a bedpan under me, transferring pressure to my neck. That was their second big mistake, the first being the bed itself.

Soon I'd lost almost all remaining sensation in my body. I knew I was dying. It was like hanging from a 10-story building by your fingertips all night. I was waiting until the 7 a.m. staff change, when Lynna would be in. I was still fighting, but with very diminished fortitude. Dying didn't seem all that bad.

My night was spent watching visions of basketball-sized primary-colored orbs dance in my room... Red, yellow, blue. Why those colors, I have no idea. I'd rather have lavender, pink, chartreuse. Then again, maybe not, since they sprang from my own mind.

Henry, the foreman at my factory job—how I paid for college—and his wife came to see me, their heads interspersed among the colored balls clouding my vision. I have no memory of their visit except that as they said goodbye, she was crying, and he said, "She isn't going to make it."

It felt like a thud, not a ping. I was resolved I would not live through the night. I just hung there by sheer will, not much feeling in my body. My mind was so very tired. I was afraid I might die and afraid I wouldn't die.

Funny what you remember.

"You look awful! What's going on?" Lynna said. I opened my eyes to look at her, but they wouldn't focus. I could not see her.

I had been trying to stay alive until she came on duty. The night nurses seemed to know something was wrong, but nobody did anything to help. But now here she was. *I made it*, I thought. *I rallied.*

"I'm on this bed upside down! I can't see, I can't breathe!"

Within about five minutes, four doctors, including Sailor, were there, a catheter was in my bladder, and a new Stryker CircOlectric bed was in the room. When I came out of the burn frame, I was out of traction. I stopped breathing again, which was the most frightening feeling of all. It burns your lungs. You hear noises, see things. Lynna had several people help make the transfer of beds. Within that hour, I was safe.

That day she became my protector—a person that you really need in a hospital setting. I would never forget her courage, sensitivity, and intelligence. She saved my life. And the only way to thank a person for something like that is to do the same for someone else.

They hooked me up, and everything changed for the better. The new bed had a circle on both sides, and you hung in a sling between them. You could be moved to any position and still be in the traction. It was what every paralyzed person needed, and I hoped others were lucky enough to have it. Even as I thought it, I told myself I was speaking for someone else—I did not plan to stay paralyzed.

The next item was that my body had not had a "removal of waste" since this all started. "They just have to go in and get it cleared," according to Saint Lynna. I stared at the ceiling in disbelief. Normally when I would go to the bathroom, I would bar the door if I could. That was over! Everything you thought could never happen does happen when you're in this situation. Not just once, but every three days.

The only part of my body that was able was my neck up, and that had the nerve to ache. Due to my head injury, I was allowed no pain medication at all. It seemed grossly unfair that the only part of my body that worked was painful. But it was also somehow reassuring. I'm not sure I would have stopped the pain if I could have.

Next up, brain surgery. *Fine,* I thought. *So what?* The thought of death did scare me, sometimes. Being calm about death was always unsettling to me. Life was such a wonderful trip; I loved so many things and people, had so many plans I wanted to see to fruition. But this was the opposite of the life I'd expected.

At times, I was also afraid of living. Brain surgery was something else. My IQ was what kept me going—work, school, my childhood had all been facilitated by my brain. Now they were poking around in there? It was terrifying. Death seemed so quiet, simple, and welcome, many times better than what lay ahead if the prognosis was true.

I did not want to live like this. How could I— why would I?

My body was asking the same questions, and in the wake of my harrowing night on the burn-frame bed, I slipped back into darkness.

I'm told I was critical and unconscious for nine days.

Chapter 3
AUGUST 1963

Hanna was standing over my bed crying as I roused. I couldn't tell if I was sleeping or conscious. I heard her as I fought to wake. "This is all my fault," she sobbed.

We'd met on our first day of factory work, when she was 18 and I was 17, her from Vienna and me from Kansas. She was married to my good friend Gary and stuck with me no matter what. She was by any standard beautiful—blond and tiny—and came from a family of beauticians. Men always grouped around Hanna, three or four at a time. She sampled the available men throughout her life, married or not, and was good to all of them, just as she was to her friends.

When we would go out barhopping, we would gladly dance with her leftovers. It was great fun. Everyone needs a friend as loving as Hanna.

"What's your fault?" I asked groggily. I think I smiled. Dr. Sailor walked in and introduced himself after telling me he was glad to see me awake again. As it would turn out, he would be no exception to the rule about men gathering around Hanna.

"I loaned you the money to go out." Her face was all stained with mascara and her nose dripped, messy. She was a "dressed to the nines" kind of person—perfect makeup, perfect hair, everything. She would normally never be seen like this. She must have really felt responsible. But it certainly was not her responsibility.

My friend had always tried to get me in line, but I was never quite as put together as she was. I did okay, though, with both men and women. Though I had tried to be straight, eventually I always returned to women. I'd been engaged to three men and had given back three rings. It was such a sad, hard thing to do, but I never wanted marriage and children. I did not want to mess up a sweet, gentle man's life. Somehow, I knew the outcome of marrying me would not be positive.

I laughed at seeing her such a mess; that made

her angry. She always had a short fuse but forgave immediately. Dr. Sailor looked at her sympathetically. Now I needed to take care of her frown. Considering my current state, I didn't have much energy to give to a woman that already had it all.

"Yeah, but Hanna, we had a really good time. We went dancing until 2 a.m." Just two drinks—a cheap night. "The money you loaned was enough. I probably can't pay you back, though. In case you haven't noticed, I took the long way home through this hospital."

She giggled, and before long, she was turning on her charming accent and man-pleasing glow. A few minutes later, she and Dr. Sailor walked out together. The heat and attraction between them was palpable. Wouldn't that be something—my best friend and my doctor?

He certainly was very attentive to my needs on the day I introduced them.

When they were gone, I went back to my safe cave, knowing Hanna and my other friends would be okay. It helped to know she was there for me and would always be there.

They scheduled me in for surgery to remove the bone shards from my brain as soon as I was awake and stable. On the big day, they came to get me at 6 a.m. Lynna was in early, with tears in her eyes. That did not help. They didn't transfer me but took the whole bed out of the room… and I was back there again by 1 p.m. I didn't feel a thing.

Ain't that the way it is? The things you fear the most sometimes turn out to be easy. I was annoyed that I'd channeled so much anxiety into this surgery for no reason. I would try to remember that as I went forward.

Dr. Waters said there was some slight damage but that I shouldn't notice any change. But I could. I was always a math person to balance my study and knowledge in psychology, and I could make an equation from most ideas. People don't know that psychology students often take their own lives. Math is a good balancing subject to prevent the application of psychology to yourself.

But I couldn't do the math now, so I noticed. And taking the splinter from my brain also took my sweet comfort cave away. I missed it dearly.

I couldn't keep drifting away to rest blissfully out of reach of the present situation. I had to stay present and farm my lot.

People began to visit, though several fainted at the sight of me. Somehow that hurt my feelings. If they seemed wobbly, I would ask them to leave. Most refused, then eventually keeled over, which pissed me off even more. My family—my mother, sister, aunts, and uncles—never visited. Why should they? I was queer! And they were Lutheran.

They did see news of the accident in the Pomona Progress-Bulletin. I guess that's something? Why they would tell me that they saw it was another question without an answer. My mother's California family and I never could connect.

Before I met Glenna, I lived in Pomona with my four favorite men: Billy, Mauricio, Kip, and Robin. Living with the boys was one of the best times of my life. We all found support and comfort there together, not to mention fun. It made us lifelong friends.

They fixed up the chicken coop in their backyard for me to live in. It was a large open room with windows all along the yard side. Kip, who worked as a designer, had painted it dark olive green and papered the walls with rice paper. The room had a high, open-beamed ceiling. It was rough but airy, beautiful when the light came through the high glass windows. Kip even made me a floor-to-ceiling fireplace, with an open-flame heater in the hearth. The boys also built me a platform for a king mattress.

I went to the high-priced carpet stores and got permission to take pieces from their dumpsters. We all used big curved needles to sew a huge patchwork carpet made of all kinds of different colorful scraps. The place turned out fantastic, right down to a tiny brick entryway patio. There was no water and no bathroom, but Mauricio charged me $10 a week for the place plus the use of their front house. Lying in my hospital bed, I yearned to return to my little coop. Though, to move Glenna from our beachfront place to my chicken coop might have been less comforting.

A young, very nice, chubby man named Sam lived next door to the Pomona house. He was a sweet, lonely man, and soon he started coming to visit me in the hospital every day, as long as they would let him stay. Sam sat there for hours each day and tried to talk with me, and I tried to be appreciative. As he talked to me, his eyes would slowly edge toward the bowl of See's Candy that had recently appeared by my bed.

Then one day, not long after the surgery, I was drifting off to sleep when a voice startled me awake. Sam had stepped out to use the bathroom. "You know, I swear he comes just for the candy."

I couldn't move my head to see who it was, but I recognized the voice immediately. For a moment, I thought I was dreaming. "Mauricio?"

"Hey, kid." His face finally came into view as he sidled up to the bed. I thought I recognized a shadow of a bruise around one of his eyes. All this time, I had counted him for dead. I had been grieving him, for Pete's sake. Yet here he was, clearly in one piece. "It's okay—you can go back to sleep."

"I'm awake now," I said. "Where have you been?" I didn't want to let on that I'd assumed he didn't make it out alive. It was too embarrassing.

"Sorry," he said. "The docs said I had to wait to see you. I'm not hurt—not really—but my face was pretty banged up. They were afraid it would upset you and make things worse."

The hot sting of anger swelled into my throat like smoke. Why had all of the staff avoided my questions when Mauricio was clearly alive and well? Though somehow, I wasn't surprised they would try to protect me in this way. I hadn't even been allowed to look at myself in the mirror since all of this began.

Mauricio sat by my bed and told me about the crash. He wanted me to know it wasn't my fault.

We'd been hit by a teenager who was going 80 miles per hour with his headlights off. I was the only one who was seriously hurt.

Mauricio's only other injuries were two chipped teeth, and the back of his pants were ripped off. The night it happened, he had walked around the hospital with his hairy ass showing and didn't know it. They kept offering him safety pins, but he declined. It wasn't until he got home that he realized his pants were missing the entire section that covered his butt.

"Don't accept a ride home with Anna," he told a nurse who was checking the various machines littered around my room. "It takes too long." We laughed like crazy. Laughter echoed in from the nurses' station down the hall. They must have heard us talking through the intercom above my bed. Clearly, they'd enjoyed the joke, too.

It was Mauricio who had planted the candy bowl on my bedside table. "To attract nurses," he said with a wink. It certainly attracted Sam; I was beginning to accept that he loved See's more than me. I finally told him to have all he wanted. I loved seeing him dig in—it was something I could do for someone.

I tried to find something for Sam to do. Eventually, Mauricio started leaving dirty magazines next to the candy bowl. Sam would stay trapped in those magazines all day. It was a relief to see him preoccupied with his candy and pinups, with no conversation needed from me.

My girlfriend, Glenna, also came every day. She was an avid reader, so she was happy to sit by the window with her book. Anything I needed was there the next day, hand-delivered by Glenna.

Glenna was a sensitive, careful person. She was close with her family—something I couldn't relate to—and had one younger brother. Most of all, she loved deeply, and somehow, I was the person she chose for a partner. Our life together was always silly, always interesting. Now she spent her days waiting for my outcome.

It helped to have two constant companions in the room. It's interesting, what lifts your spirit when you are desperate. It teaches you to hold onto this skill of seeing the positive, not out of desperation, but to be a happy, grateful person. It's a lesson I will never forget.

Now and then, a man would hover at the door to my room. He was very thin with a terse expression, and always looked like he had been crying. He wore a black suit, a black tie, and a white shirt. It made me uneasy.

I asked who this spooky guy was, but no one seemed to see him. Maybe he was part of my head injury? A relative I couldn't recognize? The nurses frequently reminded me who people were. I thought I was on top of things, but this creep made me unsure.

"Shit, I hope he's not the undertaker," I would say to Glenna. We sort of laughed, but carefully. She said he would have to wait awhile, but then looked panicked, afraid she had misspoken. People always tried so hard to do and say the right thing. Once, Glenna was running late and told me she "broke her neck to get there." Then she burst into tears.

"He's more like the corpse," she offered.

One day he entered the room. "Welcome," I said. He did not make eye contact. "Do I know you? You've been outside my room for several days now."

He seemed relieved. "I'm Dr. Bullox," he offered, looking at the shiny tile floor. "I've been assigned to you for your adjustment phase."

"Could you look at me?" I asked. "I'm in traction. Adjustment to what?" Finally, his gaze found mine, but only for a second. His watery blue eyes slipped to the floor again.

His chin quivered. He looked miserable, maybe the palest person I'd ever met without Halloween makeup on. Maybe it was the black suit.

"Quadriplegic living," he whispered.

"I was already told—you can say the word. It's okay." He relaxed just a fraction. "You don't seem to be comfortable with this," I challenged carefully, feeling slightly annoyed. "Seems I need to do something to help you?" His discomfort was unmistakable. Sam and Glenna decided to take a walk, Sam's candy jar in tow.

Jeez, where do they get these people? Is he the only psych in Pomona? I thought. *Maybe I could work here as a runner—I should find out who does the hiring. They would never know I can't actually run!*

Whoops—I had to be careful not to get too used to the idea of staying in that bed.

"You're the first broken neck at PVH. It's new to all of us," Bullox stammered.

"I'm still just a person, aren't I? Does my injury change everything for you?" I asked.

"It does," he said. "How do I help you?" He had started to cry.

My heart fell to my neck. (That's all I could feel. HA.) Was it possible that he felt worse about my situation than I did? In some eerie way that made me feel lifted. But his incompetence made me wonder. Maybe if he couldn't help me, I could help him.

"Okay, Dr. Bullox. Let's do this." And so we started "How to Be a Quad 101." *Stupid*, I thought—I was not going to live like this—but there was nothing else to busy my mind. At least it would take up some time. I thought of it as entertainment, and though I didn't know it then, it turned out to be one of the best things offered to me.

Dr. Bullox started by telling me about himself— an unusual start. At the time, I was fresh out of school and needed to write a dissertation for my PhD if I ever managed to return. So as he introduced himself, I surmised he needed help and decided I would turn our sessions toward his sadness and away from mine. I had no intention of adjusting to the mess I was caught within. He was divorcing; he was as close to suicide as I was. The difference was that he could do it on his own, whereas I needed help. Maybe we could be strangers on the train, if it came to it.

"So, Doctor," I said. "Tell me more about your wife."

He told me how he felt he'd failed her and that they were still together but actively contemplating a split. They had no children to complicate matters. I latched onto his pain as a way of avoiding my own.

From then on, our three meetings each week would become a healthy distraction. He was, in my never-to-be-humble opinion, the most ineffective therapist I would ever meet. But he was also a really nice man. I think I was able to help him, and that profoundly helped me.

All was fine until he billed me months later. I wrote across the invoice, YOU OWE ME. DO NOT BILL AGAIN.

He never did.

Chapter 4

Dr. Bullox did help me come to terms with a change in thinking. Because I could help him, I felt more able. It was not his intent, but the part of me that still worked could be useful.

Before Bullox, I had a plan to quit life. I had the pills but no way to take them without involving another person. Since that's called murder, I couldn't ask that of anyone. Or could I?

I decided to wait until I could do it myself somehow. It seemed most things now were "waits"—wait for a nurse to come by, wait for food. Most usual bodily processes just happened, though. There was no wait there, just humiliation.

The staff did their best, saying this work was what they wanted to do, what they'd signed up for. I couldn't really adjust.

My view consisted of one ceiling tile, the large acoustic type with random pinholes in it. And those tiny holes were maddening. It seems if your mind finds it has nothing to do, it tries to make designs of dots on the ceiling. To make me feel even nuttier, I had a nice window but could never quite see out of it because my head was held straight by the traction. *You can do anything for a while,* I said to myself many times a day.

Nights were my escape from those damn ceiling dots. The fact that I am very nearsighted helped. There aren't enough numbers to express how many times it would have been cathartic to just scream. They actually call that "chaotic meditation," and believe it or not, it works. But not in a hospital setting. The way people come running to help you tends to ruin the relief.

At times, I would notice people at my door. One day, someone at the side of my vision came into my room. The way she moved made me think she wasn't supposed to be there. Dressed in a floral cotton robe, she sort of glided up next to my bed. For the first time, I realized I was completely unprotected; if someone wanted to hurt me, they could. Just a pillow over my face would do it. The thought didn't frighten me, though; something about a dramatic exit was appealing. But it had never occurred to me that it might be at the hands of a stranger in a floral robe.

I turned toward her as best I could and smiled. She was a woman of about 45 years, with long natural blond hair pulled back, and tears running down a puffy, kind-looking face. She must have been tall because I could see her from my face-up position. *Oh Christ,* I thought. *Do I know this person? Is it my head injury?*

She finally spoke in a deep, raspy voice. "I'm Mrs. Willowby. Room 110, across the hall."

"Okay," I stammered. As she stood there, I realized the nurses had told me about her two days ago. Mrs. Willowby and another patient, Mr. Tallow, were found in bed together by the night nurse in a... compromising position. According to my sources, it happened more often than you think. Hospital gossip was the best.

She continued, "My daughter was in a car accident. She wasn't hurt half as bad as you. But she never recovered."

I apologized, trying to console her, and wondered aloud if her daughter was also a quad. Mrs. Willowby didn't answer. She just stood there, flat-footed, blank-faced, sobbing.

Her nose was running. I was keenly focused that it not drip on me. I had no more words, so I just looked up at her until she abruptly turned and left.

For several weeks, Mrs. Willowby came every morning to cheer me with her message. At times, I would even cry with her. It was something I could count on each day. I wondered if she still saw her sexy Mr. Tallow.

Then came the day that my sweet Dr. Jack Sailor, orthopedic specialist, would stick me in a Minerva cast. Though he was delighted with his idea, I had no clue what was coming on that rainy morning. We were all about to find out.

Dr. Sailor looked more like a happy mechanic than an ortho doctor, and I loved that about him. He had curly dark hair that was too long, and it fell over his forehead in Eddie Fisher style. (Look him up.) His white coat was not quite white. He carried pliers and sundry tools in his pockets and greeted you as though he wanted to sell you something. He ran, seldom walked, and was built like a boxer. Lately, he sported a deep tan.

Hadn't I noticed Hanna's tan was deeper than usual recently, too?

Plus, he was listed in a ratings magazine as one of the top orthopedic doctors in the US—lucky, lucky me! (This fact was offered up by one of the night nurses, Faith, who fed me goodies and spent time with me during those long nights. She had an obvious crush on Sailor. It seemed he did not disappoint his admirers.)

On the appointed day, I was taken to the large operating room with a window and viewing area looking in at one end. We all chatted and told jokes as I was rolled through the hall. I was removed from my beloved circle bed and placed on a stool that looked like a piano bench. Inexplicably, it had rollers. A group of people were to hold me in a sitting position. That seemed chancy, but I was no expert. What could go wrong?

Just about everything, honestly. Holding a limp, six-foot-tall woman on a rolling stool—sure, why not? It seemed to me like a comedy routine, and I could already see the people around me filled with tension. Staring at their widening eyes, full of anticipation, did not help me "relax" as they repeatedly requested that I do.

While the top ortho doctor in the country prepared to wrap me in plaster—again, nothing worked on my body except my head—the scene didn't look too great to that head. I sat there, stark nude, at six feet tall and 150 pounds with a noodle body, with the traction attached to my skull and tied to the overhead light fixture. I tried to focus on the lighted window at the end of the operating room. We had attracted a small crowd of people to watch our impending fiasco.

Dr. Sailor said, "If anything hurts, tell me." My vision was getting a little wonky. *Was that a joke?* I thought. *If I felt anything, I think we would celebrate!*

"Okay," I said, looking into his eyes. He looked relaxed and confident, much more so than my stabilizer team. It reminded me of a scene from M*A*S*H. They always did things casually, too. I suppose that made sense, since Sailor was a military doc.

Then the stool's wheels slipped from under me, and the people holding me said "Oops!" all at once. The stool was retrieved and so was I, and I was placed on that damn rolling seat again with my traction still in my head and the light fixture swinging wildly. Sweat was pouring off me, so they had to turn up the air conditioning and try to wipe me down. It was the first time I'd been up in days. I was crying, and so were two of my support team. Dr. Sailor's shoulders were tense—tenser than I would have liked.

The room was spinning now, and my head felt explosive. Some rational thought passed through my mind. *Am I having a stroke?*

"I'm going to throw up," I whispered.

Sailor calmly said, "No, you aren't."

I didn't. And by now, I could see many people at the observation window again. They were lit from behind, like when you first see the aliens in a space movie. One of the shadows seemed to notice my attention on them. They raised a fist—a sign of solidarity or of defiance? From my completely passive position down below, it seemed off. *No defiance here*, I thought.

I couldn't have cared less about them. I was too alarmed about my real or imaginary stroke. But Sailor assured me there was none. As usual, I wanted to rely on my own opinion, so panic persisted nonetheless.

It was time to temporarily disconnect my traction. "This is a sock that goes under the cast," Sailor said as it was slipped over my head among the scramble of hands and arms holding my limp body. Then they were reattaching the traction at his command. I truly had no control over anything. I think I now understood exactly what being paralyzed really meant.

I wanted to cry, but I couldn't, and the noises that came from me sounded like a wounded animal. A stroke seemed more appealing.

This was not like the pristine, precise surgeries on TV. "Who's on first?" I shouted as the light fixture continued to swing. I kept going over and over into my exhausted thoughts, trying to adjust to this scene, trying to retreat into my cave of unconsciousness. Finally, I settled into the helpless conclusion that none of these people knew what they were doing.

"Now the plaster wrap. You're doing great," Sailor assured, bending to make eye contact with me. My "support staff" did a collective sigh. The whole ordeal was like trying to hold onto a slippery fish. My part, sadly, was being the fish.

The room spun around and so did the people at the window. "Stay with me," he instructed. I tried. By now, my holding troupe was all standing, in proof of my fear and lack of control. *God, please take me now,* I thought. *I can't do this.*

In that moment, dying in that street seemed a better outcome. It was as though my sense of self was being destroyed bit by bit. The usual resistance that had sustained me until now was fading.

And then I was back in my room wrapped in

damp, warm plaster tape. It was all over my head and upper body. The feeling of being confined, of being unable to breathe in the soggy cast, only added to my complete failure of will.

"Please, can I have something to knock me out?"

"No, sorry," the staff told me. No pain meds allowed. The nurses felt as helpless as I did, and two of them stood by my bedside and cried with me that night. I was in deep, jarring pain, though I could feel none. It's very hard to explain. Almost like careening untethered down a warm, slick rockslide. No control. No hope.

That night was my first panic attack. And I now understood claustrophobia, unfortunately.

(Note to self: be more sympathetic with others.)

7 a.m. again. "How are you feeling?" Lynna said. "Your blood pressure is off the chart! I've called Sailor, and he's on his way over. He's just across the street."

She stayed in my room, not talking and just being present. Nothing she could have said would have changed the moment.

The cast was mostly dry but still felt too close

to my body. I had never been a sweaty person, but I was now. More pressing was that I couldn't open my jaw because the plaster was forcing it shut, and Lynna said it was now bleeding onto the cast. The pain was all I could think and feel. My head was held tight in the cast, and I couldn't get relief by moving. It felt like utter defeat.

Dr. Sailor popped in the door, pliers in hand. *So that's what they're used for*, I thought. He put his knees on the bed, leaned on my deadweight body and, in four quick moves, cracked the chin part of the cast. The pain was instantly gone.

I was so angry. "Why the hell do I wait in pain all night until Lynna comes?"

He looked at me with soft brown eyes. "We're all here to help you, Anna." He had a crisp, clean smock, neatly combed hair, a freshly shaved face, and a brilliant smile. He even smelled like mint. As I looked at him, I realized how tattered I must look in contrast. My anger intensified.

"It's fixed now," he whispered. Then he said, "You didn't tell anyone it was cutting into you. Don't be stoic—say something if you're hurting."

I was doing my best to look furious, but I think I just looked pathetic. "The blood didn't give a hint?! Or how about my tears, or my pleas for a pain pill?"

I was serious, but Sailor read humor in my words. "That sarcasm just might pull you out of this," he joked. Try as I might, I couldn't stay angry at him. His easy banter made me want to giggle.

Suddenly, we were all laughing in that uncontrolled, catch your breath way. The doctor wiped his eyes and said, "That was a good one. I think we all needed a laugh." He paused. "But please, Anna. Tell us what you need. We can't always know on our own."

What a circus, I thought. *I will never live through this.* And my tears of laughter turned to sorrow. He looked at me, understanding my plight.

As he turned and left my room, I thought to myself that the grave difference was that I could not. I was in this damp, warm cast, tied to a bed by my head. It was like I had almost ceased to exist.

And he went back across the street to complete his day.

Chapter 5

Someone was just inside my room, knocking on the doorframe. Thanks to the cast and the traction, I couldn't turn to look at them. "Hello?" I called.

"Hi, Anna," said a voice that sounded vaguely familiar. After a few moments, a man's face entered the limited halo of my vision. A pair of sea green eyes looked down at me, a tinge of sadness coloring their gaze. For a moment, I thought it might be another Mrs. Willowby—just someone satiating their morbid curiosity. But he must have clocked my lack of recognition, because he added, "I'm Trevor. From the street?"

Suddenly, it clicked. It was my kind stranger—the man who had sung to me as I lay bleeding on the pavement. No wonder I hadn't known who he was. I'd never seen his face that night because my sight kept blinking in and out. "Oh my God, Trevor. It's so wonderful to see you," I said, breathless. "Please, sit!"

He dropped into a chair and rubbed a few nervous circles on his knees with his palms, seemingly unsure what to do with his hands. "I can't tell you how glad I am that you're alive and talking. With the state you were in, well... I've been praying for you, but I assumed I wouldn't be seeing you again."

"I probably have you to thank for that. But I don't remember much of what happened, really," I told him. "Just waking up on the asphalt and hearing your voice."

His face tightened into a look of anguish. "I saw the whole thing. So did a bunch of other people; there were three cars sitting in that intersection." He explained how they had all witnessed the 16-year-old barrel into the junction, headlights off, as I was turning on a green light. He had been in the middle of his paper route. Thankfully, the boy had escaped without so much as a scratch.

"When I saw you and your passenger on the ground, at first I thought you were just bundles of cloth or something that had been thrown out of the car when it got hit." Trevor gulped. "I never imagined it was bodies. Not until I got closer and saw the blood."

Judging by the deep crease of his brow, I knew it could not have been an easy thing to witness. Did he have dreams about that night that left him panting in a cold sweat? Though I was the only person who'd found myself in a hospital bed, I felt certain I was not the only person who'd been scarred by the crash.

"I'm lucky you were there to call for help," I said quietly.

"I was a little hurt, if I'm honest." One corner of his mouth turned up in a teasing, sad smile. "As soon as the ambulance arrived, you dropped my hand like it was a hot coal."

That made me laugh. "I guess I was a little preoccupied in the moment. I'm sure I can find some way to make it up to you."

Trevor sat with me for nearly an hour, telling me all about what he'd seen and how it made him feel. I was grateful that he was there to make sense of the holes in my memory, but at the same time, I was grief-stricken that we had been forced to enter each other's lives in this way.

"Goodbye, Anna," he said as he turned to go. "I'll keep saying my prayers."

As the days went by, routine took over. At 6 a.m., they took my vitals, and someone would feed me a small breakfast. Then it was bath time, followed by a daily sheet change and an enema every three days. The nurses spent time with me when they could. I looked forward to the stories about their lives and the hospital gossip. They kept me willing to continue; they were what kept the hospital going.

I was often surprised by everything they were juggling on the outside—husbands, children, money problems, parents, lovers, their own health issues. Listening to them, in many ways, can help diminish your intense attention on the self. Hospital life is all about self until it isn't.

Though most of my routine ran like a well-oiled machine, lunch was a real problem. The nurse that was assigned to feed me regularly stuffed the food into my mouth until I couldn't breathe. Once it actually came out of my nose. I'd ask her to slow down, but she wouldn't. I hated the bitch. Eventually, I stopped eating lunch and soon had to explain the reason to my caretakers. They were shocked.

I discussed it with Hanna, and she started

coming every day to feed me. When I told Lynna, she said the girl was forced to feed me during her own lunch hour and had taken it out on me. Lynna was, of course, livid this happened and even offered to cover lunches herself. If you look up nurse in the dictionary, Lynna's picture should be there. She wasn't my only dedicated caretaker, but I know I am here today because of her efforts to keep me alive.

After that, I asked to see Killer Nurse and told her, "I will get out of this bed. I will find out where you live and repay you for trying to hurt me." At first she looked embarrassed, then petulant.

She was a sort of attractive, curvy woman of about my age with dark, curly hair. She was very pale and had a spotty complexion covered by makeup. Her eyes were sad, watery, and bright blue. She always seemed angry.

"It wasn't my fault," she insisted.

I really did not like her, and that felt good— it gave me a place to put some of my fury. I thought I could match her level of animosity. We glared at each other like it was the O.K. Corral. I needed somewhere to channel my anger, and she presented a grand target.

"You had the spoon," I said. "Your job is to help patients, and instead you tried to hurt me. I wouldn't be surprised if you had put others at risk, too. Maybe someone should look at the deaths in this hospital when you were on duty."

Eyes wide, she looked right into my face and said, "You will never get out of that bed. So I don't care what you think you can do—it will never touch me. You can stay there until you rot for all I care, you queer bitch."

Shocked into silence, I stared as she turned on her heel and left. Her response was not "Sorry," not "Forgive me," just "Fuck you." Most of the people who cared for me went way beyond what was expected to do the best they could. This woman should have never been allowed near a patient.

It seemed to me, everyone knew what she was like.

My afternoons were visiting with Sam, who came each day to be kind and eat candy. Glenna came most days between noon and 5 p.m., and she'd stay until after my dinner. She never let me down. I kept asking about bills, money, the fact that she was not working. She assured me she was okay, things were okay. Part of me felt uneasy, but I loved her presence there, so why push it?

There was a flurry of activity at about 6 p.m.

before the night shift started at 7 p.m. Vitals, charge sheets, lotion, checking my body's pressure points. Lights out. Over and over, day after day. I guess we all go through our little rituals each night. But the hospital made the daily cycle feel more boring—more mind-numbing.

I usually slept, but there was one streetlight that shined through the window right in my eyes. It couldn't move, and I couldn't move. It was like a game of chicken; just me and that damn streetlight, every night. Finally, I asked to move my bed, but it wasn't possible with all the equipment in my room.

The nurses found the spot on the window and placed a scratchpad sheet of paper over it—relief. But nearly every visitor walked over to the window and removed the blank paper scotch-taped in that seemingly random location. It just bothered people. Silly. Even if I said not to, they still took it down, and then the nurse would replace it. And on and on the little game continued until we finally put a note on it.

"Do not remove this fucking piece of paper."

One night it was 7 p.m.—no more visitors—and in walked a stunning woman. Seldom do I ever look at someone and POW! But this was different. I was so drawn to her without one spoken word. I don't like men or women that ogle at attractive people, gay or straight. But when I saw her, I became that person.

"Good evening. My name is Vonetta Radcliff. You're my patient tonight," she said. I stared at her. She understood, smiling. "How are you? I hear you're the hit of Pomona South."

She was teasing me. Maybe she felt sorry for me. How could anyone be attracted to a person in an electric bed, accessorized with metal tongs and a Minerva cast, only really available from the neck up?

She had bright, clear blue eyes and striking red hair. Her uniform was crisp, ironed, and very white. Some of the nurses' frocks were a little dumpy, but not Radcliff's. Everything about this woman fit perfectly, from her hair and makeup to her watch. I felt shy, which was unusual for me. There was something about the way her body moved—smoothly, like a dancer. She wasn't exactly beautiful, but she looked flawless to me.

Radcliff rolled in and took charge. When she touched me, going about her checks and measurements, it was in places I could feel and, shamefully, my mind gave in to my attraction. I was so delighted just to feel something, some kind of titillation, and my own reaction took me by surprise. It was a blessing, and I selfishly signed up for what I could get.

From my position in that bed, why not? There was none of my usual consideration, just plain lust. I was safe in my paralysis. Finally, a use for this unholy situation. I had to laugh at myself. You could say I was taking the idea of making lemonade out of lemons to the extreme.

By then, the staff in the hospital either knew I was gay or thought I had befriended the most select cast of "interesting" characters in the place. I had to admit that, at a time when even the hint of being a lesbian would cause you to lose your job, most of them took it in stride.

That first night, Radcliff told me that the nurses would leave the intercom speaker in my room turned on and listen in. "They love your visitors. They listen and laugh along with all of you," she said. "They're all surprised at how much they like you. Hell, they love the men the most."

Recently, my old roommates had started to bring food to the nurses' station. Mauricio was an excellent chef, and his Mexican cooking was a favorite. He brought a large basket filled with sweet bread and tortillas every Monday, his day off from the She She Beauty Shop where he worked. There were never any leftovers.

"They don't know about me," Radcliff continued. Her complexion turned bright pink. "I asked to be put on your case. But if they suspect an attraction or that I'm being 'off-color' with you, I'll lose my job."

"I didn't know either," I offered. "Thanks for going to the trouble. I feel safer now with you here. It's like having a family member nearby."

"Sure you knew! I could tell," she laughed. "They know I drink too much, but that's okay. Being gay wouldn't be. So you and your friends had better go easy on me."

I understood, reassuring her that we would be careful. This was the reality in 1963. I knew my visitors would be as cautious and concerned about protecting her privacy as she was.

"The girl that fed you lunch and choked you," she said softly, "she knows."

"What do you mean?"

She locked her crystal blue eyes on me. "She knows about me. And about you."

I was both shocked and furious in one moment. "Are you... Were you with her?" She didn't answer, looking concerned and avoiding my eyes.

"No games, please," I told her. I couldn't quite

see her from my position in the bed.

Radcliff moved closer to look at me. "What's with you and Lynna? She really went to bat with your safety."

"Really?" was all I could reply. Lynna had saved my ass so many times already. I was hoping to keep her as a friend when this was over. "She's a professional, like you—a nurse. I'm sure her only concern is my physical welfare."

The idea of Lynna factoring into this type of conversation left me feeling shaken. What if it tarnished her reputation somehow?

"Is the woman Glenna your partner?" Vonetta asked, after a beat. "She's very loyal—always here. She doesn't work?"

"I'm not sure that's your concern." I realized she was just finding her footing, but I bristled. My fantasy was taking on the disquieting cloud of reality.

"Yes, she's my partner," I answered after a moment. "She's the best person I have ever met. We've been together two years. We live together but we have an open agreement—nonmonogamous." I didn't mention that the arrangement wasn't really working for Glenna. "If I wanted to be married, I would be with a man."

We had even written the agreement down and signed it. It outlined that we would both be free to have sexual relationships outside of our partnership, that we would keep our money separate, and that whoever made the higher salary would put their name on the lease. It was sort of like a prenup, without the nuptials. But as we approached our third year together, Glenna started to want a change. I did not, nor did I make this clear to Radcliff. I felt it didn't involve her.

Radcliff gave me a look, noting my eyes lingering on her figure. "So you must be a bit of a jerk, right?" She chuckled and moved to the side of my bed, touching my cheek.

I took my eyes away. If that's how it was, why not tell the truth?

"If this is part of keeping me going, it's working," I confided.

"Yes, I can tell," she said dangerously. "Me too."

"Then, yes, I guess I am a bit of a jerk," I said, sheepish. "But don't you think I'm rather out of business at the moment anyway? So if you'd be willing to have a little fun banter, I'd love it. As you can tell, it's giving me a feather to hang onto."

"Me too," she beamed. "I need a reason to come to work, and I think you're it. That's why I transferred to you. Both of us needs the other. We'll find out together what this could be."

I held her eyes with mine. "We can see how

this goes. The responsibility to Glenna is mine alone," I told her. "You're a whole different song. And so far, I love the way your music feels."

If anyone would have told me, "Don't," I would have rolled my eyes in disbelief. But there it was. It lifted my spirit as nothing else could. Finding new interest really changes perspective. The sun looks brighter. Your mood feels lighter. You can look forward.

I did consider Glenna, but I never mentioned it to her, as we'd agreed I would not. She would never think of this happening, especially not in a hospital room, between a nurse and a patient, and a paralyzed patient at that. But it did.

So now, five days a week at 7 p.m., Vonetta Radcliff would come on stage and the curtain would open on the night show. I loved the boost it gave me. Guilt? Nope—none. Maybe she was a planted part of my transition therapy. Who cares? If so, it was very successful!

It was exactly what I needed when I needed it. My life has always been that way, unsurprisingly. I somehow felt blessed, protected—that eventually I would get up and walk away, though I didn't know when or how. For a moment there, I thought I had lost my angel, but no. She was still there, looking out for me. She'd seen me through a hard childhood, getting through college the tough way, going it alone far too often. Even if she was just some chemical surge of confidence inside my mind, she was clearly still available to me.

Now my days were better. The nursing staff had set up my schedule of care, food, and visitors, and it seemed we had my life worked out for now. I felt secure and happy most days knowing what to expect, without many surprises. I asked Glenna to bring in an eight-by-ten-inch picture of me, because I wanted all the people I could relate with to know how I looked inside the cast, out of this bed. It was the first professional photograph I had ever had taken, originally intended as a headshot for my budding clinical practice.

My room was filled with laughter as my friends would visit over the week. The nurses, aides, physical therapists, lab technicians, and of course, my adjustment psych, Dr. Bullox, were accepting of my visitors and learned their names. It was a type of family. Each person found something I needed and gave me what they could. I worried I could not return the favor. I would turn out to be right about that; I would never be able to repay what they'd offered me.

Maybe it was a relief for them to have me entertained, but I think they met us as intelligent, kind, and loving people instead of as queers and faggots. In the '60s, that was a rare concept.

I felt positive in a small way that we could make a difference.

Chapter 6
SEPTEMBER 1963

Mrs. Willowby came to visit at about 9 a.m. She was crying—what was new? She took my hand. I hated that; my arm looked and felt like a piece of stuff not connected to me. Seeing my arm but not feeling it always made me upset, spreading a funny sick feeling through me. Whenever people needed to handle my body, I tried not to look.

If she doesn't stop doing that, I thought, *I'll ask that she not come to my room.* She meant no harm, but she couldn't seem to listen to my request. Her daily message had now become a well-circulated joke in the hospital. Her daughter was not hurt half as bad as me—"she never recovered."

When Lynna returned after her latest day off, I asked to have her banned. "Are you talking about Iris Willowby across the hall?"

I nodded.

"She died last night, so your problem is solved." Lynna was so matter of fact. *Someday she'll be saying the same about me*, I thought. *No problem, my patient Anna finally died.* My stomach was an elevator descending much too fast.

My sadness lasted for several days. Everyone was asking what had happened. It was like I truly got it—my lot came into clear focus and, finally, I was terrified. This was real. I was not going to get out of this bed, this room, this hospital. This was my "it."

"Why aren't you eating?" a nurse said one day at dinnertime.

Mauricio answered for me. "She doesn't want to split her cast by gaining too much weight."

His silly, high-camp voice pierced my sad fog. "Yeah, not an option." I laughed halfheartedly. Whenever a crack opened in the dark container that enveloped me, Mauricio could usually slip some light through. He was the one person that could visit and just sit with me without trying to say the correct thing or constantly entertain. I thanked God it was my neck that had broken and not his. The thought of his hairy body sweltering in that cast was unbearable.

My melancholy was not helped by the fact that, after a while, it seemed Radcliff was not on my room assignment as often. She would ask to take the shift, but was told no. The sadness I felt was extreme, and the idea I could cause her problems haunted me. Things always change, but I hoped this would be an exception. I feared the worst, and unfortunately, I was right.

One day, an aide entered the room. "Oh, it looks like someone left an empty hypodermic needle here from your last pain shot," she said.

I blinked. "But I don't get pain shots."

"Yes, you do. You don't remember?"

Being questioned this way—as if I were a child who couldn't keep track of her own shoes—always set my blood boiling. They said they had to look me over for needle marks, but found none, of course. After a big commotion in the hallway, I gathered that they thought one of the nurses had taken drugs. I would later discover that they suspected Radcliff of stealing them for herself.

Apparently, the nurses' desk was still listening on the intercom and had some questions about things that were discussed in my room. It seems they thought I was influencing Radcliff, so they decided to keep her out. And they were concerned about Lynna, too. Clearly the specter of queerphobic proselytizing was still lurking in the halls of PVH. But to cover their asses by accusing drug theft? What a mess. I felt responsible. Lynna mentioned suing them once, but she never brought it up again.

I missed Radcliff, but there was nothing to be done right then without too much attention attached. Lynna told the other nurses to stuff it, that the rumors about me and Radcliff were not true, and they believed her. After all, Radcliff was a married woman. We all giggled about that. *Oh yeah, no married woman or man would ever go out with a gay person.* It's just so silly—people do that all the time. Though Lynna probably wouldn't. I felt sad that she'd been questioned because of me. But she just said, "Oh, get over it—it was stupid, nothing that mattered."

Still, Radcliff would drop by at times. She had been suspended briefly, but the hospital was forced to reinstate her when her drug tests came back negative. We kept it very middle of the road, but it always lifted my day. She suggested trying to rig a phone so we could talk. But at that time, it couldn't be done without hands, and the nurses could listen in on the line if they wanted to.

Then one day, Radcliff was in my room at 7 p.m. She said I had been assigned as her patient, with no reason given. So my evening improved, but with reservations—I didn't want to cause her another problem. The visitors were delighted to see her, almost like a homecoming.

She thought Lynna had pull with her assignment. We wondered what that woman had on people, and we were happy she was on our side. Lynna only cared about my welfare and never took any other position.

It was her job; she was a nurse.

The day, to day, to day, to day had become almost more than I could bear. At times, there was so much pressure in my head it was intolerable. I couldn't cry; I wanted to scream. It was sort of a constant, dull panic attack. One thing was for certain: I needed a change.

I thought about the stories I had read about people found completely burned to ashes; spontaneous human combustion, they called it. Maybe it would happen to me. My bed would be there, and I would be nothing but a pile of ash on the sheets. It sounded good to me! The idea was probably closer to fiction than reality, but a quad could hope.

Desperate for relief, I tried to meditate. I had learned about the practice while I was working toward my degree. Normally, I'd have preferred to sit with my feet flat on the floor and my arms resting on my legs. But since I was stuck in my bed, lying down would have to do. I leaned my head back as much as I could, closed my eyes, and began to breathe.

In through the nose. Out through the mouth. In. Out. I repeated the exercise ten times, focusing on lengthening my breaths and willing myself to escape into my own mind. I was free within that space and could visit any place, go where I pleased. As my focus sharpened, I made a mental list of special memories to revisit.

The first try was to a place on my Uncle Frank and Aunt Fern's farm in Kansas, on the prairie. It was the one place where I always felt peaceful, safe, and free. That was not the experience of most of my childhood, which was spent being shuffled around to relatives, friends, and a few strangers. The farm was a huge expanse of wheat, so many acres that it took an hour to get off the property.

Every day after chores, my sister and I could run wild. We walked out the back door, across a large lawn, and into the barnyard past the three barns: one for equipment, the next for feed and supplies, and then the barn where we hand milked the four cows. It all smelled like sweet hay. The pigpen was last, far enough to let the wind take that scent away. They knew us, squealing their greeting, and we loved them right back. Pigs are very smart, my uncle always said. "Smarter than dogs." They could also be dangerous if their piglets were threatened. The piglets were my favorite— darling little creatures.

We lived with Uncle Frank and Aunt Fern for a good amount of time. Aside from being so good to two little girls that needed love, they also kept a sterling clean farm for their animals. Yes, they were grown for food, but right up to the end, they were carefully and humanely cared for—and humanely killed. Past the pigs, there was another hill and then the bottom gate. "Be sure to latch the gate, girls," came my uncle's sweet reminder. We always did.

"Are you okay, Anna?" a nurse interrupted. I jumped, startled back to my hospital room. After she jumped, too, we just stared at one another. I laughed first, then she dissolved into snorting giggles.

"Yes, I'm okay," I finally choked out. "Just learning to meditate. I tried to visit a childhood farm."

"Oh, great idea," she replied. "Do you need anything?" I declined, and the room melted away again.

I was emerging from our barnyard into the ocean of sweet-scented grass we called the open prairie. It was a hot day, so we decided to go to the willow tree swimming hole. We trudged along, up over a bluff, and stopped to enjoy the view. The sky was bright blue with big fluffy clouds. We liked to find animals and people in their shapes.

When people mention Kansas or the prairie, they often smirk. "Oh, how flat, so dry, what long drives." In reality, it's not like that at all. There are plenty of rolling hills, sharp drop bluffs, and many cricks flowing deep and fast into large ponds. I always loved the prairie.

"Think it might rain," I said aloud. The wind seemed to have switched direction and become damper, slightly cooler.

"NO!" my little sister said, blond locks bobbing. Carla was 18 months younger than me, a headstrong girl then about five years old. She took no crap from her teasing older sister. She always could beat me up. *Still seems like rain to me*, I thought to myself.

We basked in the hot sun, the wonderful scent of grass, the ever-present breeze on our faces. We stepped into the swimming hole and let the water cover our heads—aaahhhhhh... It was so cool and refreshing. It was chiseled out of a small stream bed, with a muddy, rocky bottom. The stream was home to a few fish and crawdads, maybe one catfish. We both knew how to swim, but we just floated, soaking in all the day offered, savoring the contrast between walking under a hot sun and dropping into shady water.

The tree let its branches down into the water like slender fingers, creating a sort of shaded cave in the weeping willow hands. We loved the familiar spot. It was always cool there—quiet and safe. The smell of a willow—a scent like no other tree—will always take me back to that swimming hole. Once you soak it in, you never forget it. It was a little extra comfort for two little girls who needed it very much.

We stayed in the grass under the cover of the old willow tree's branches until the sun was straight overhead. "When the sun hits high noon, you girls must turn to home," my aunt would say. We always obeyed, though we also believed that the better we behaved, the longer we could stay.

A tray banged on my bed table. "Time for lunch," the kitchen delivery person said. "Are you awake?" The dietitian, a large, tall woman with a jovial smile, came to my room every day to see what she could cook for me. I was so touched she would go to that trouble. I usually had some ideas for her, and she seemed delighted that I liked the food. Later, I found out I was the only patient that received such a special service. I was overcome with gratitude.

Just then, Hanna walked into my room. "Hi! Ready to eat?" she said in her soft, high voice. My friend always seemed ready for a chat and never once acted put upon to come visit every day at noon. I know at times it was inconvenient for her.

"Yes," I said. "I want to tell you where I've been." I dove into the story of my new escape—the farm, the animals, the feeling of the sun and the breeze, the coolness of the swimming hole. She tried to smile, but I saw sadness behind her eyes.

She looked confused. "Really?" she said in her charming accent. "Are you sure you're alright? Do you have a fever? I've heard..." Her voice trailed off.

"I can go anyplace I want," I said. "I learned to meditate. My mind can get out of this bed." It was such a relief.

When she still looked like she wanted to cry,

I tried to explain again what meditation was.

"Oh," she said finally. "Nachdenken in German? Is that what you mean?"

I nodded, delighted, but Hanna still seemed unsure. The concept of meditation was not as widely accepted in the West then as it is now. "Do your doctors think it's a good thing?" she asked.

"Of course. What can it hurt?"

"Nothing, I suppose." Hesitance was still written across her face, but she looked less concerned now. She picked up a spoon and carefully opened my food and her own. Today was ground beef and mashed potato. "It looks good," she observed, raising the spoon to take a bite.

The kitchen always made enough for her, too—Lynna's pull again! Several people had apologized for what happened with the other nurse and tried to make lunch an extra nice time. I was really starting to realize how lucky I was to be at PVH. Good old McDaniel thought I should be sent to Los Angeles County Hospital. Instead, Sailor and Waters kept me near my friends. It was the first time I was ever in the hospital, and things could have been much less personal; I realized how catered to I actually was. And it was still the worst event of my life.

After lunch and a chat with Hanna, it was time

for body maintenance, as they called it. Then I was free to "leave." Sam was still there, flipping through his magazines and eating See's Candy, and Glenna was engrossed in her book. I was anxious to return to the farm. The window by my bed was open, and as a breeze whispered over my face, my ceiling tile began to fade...

We slowly walked back toward home, in no hurry today because we didn't go far. Suddenly, we noticed a large black snake across our path. He was three feet long and quite beautiful; clean and shiny. He looked at us from his sunny spot with small yellow eyes, and finally he seemed to decide we would not harm him. Uncle Frank's words came to mind: "Don't ever kill a black snake—they eat rats." We carefully stepped over him. It was evident by the lump in his body that he had a lucky hunt today. On our free-to-roam days, we would often see a bobcat, coyote, or deer, all from a distance, usually as they ran from us. I never felt afraid there.

"Can we go see the prairie dogs?" my sister asked. She loved our spot at the prairie dog camp, as we called it. The swath of land where they lived was large and well-populated. They were used to us and would always sound the alert that we'd arrived, but then go on with their daily chores. We found them fascinating, especially the way they taught their young the order of things. I liked how they cooperated to stay safe and find food, and would seldom fight. Eventually, my sister finally realized they were not fighting after all but engaging in something more scandalous to our young eyes.

"Not today, Carla, it'll make us late. Maybe tomorrow." Neither of us wanted to worry our aunt and uncle. We loved them and the farm too much.

We did stop at the bluff to look over the valley. As we sat there in the early afternoon sun, the wind changed, and suddenly you could feel the extra dampness on the breeze. Lightning spread across the sky way out on the horizon. If I could have stayed there forever, I would have. The smell of rain on the wind was delicious, but then the lightning, thunder, and pounding hail would follow.

On the prairie, you can witness the rain come down in gray sheets from a long way off. First you feel the wind shift, a welcome thing on a hot Kansas day. The wall of water advances toward you, then a whisper of thunder, a flash of lightning. If you don't race the storm home, the pouring rain will be overhead and pounding down.

"Come on, Carla, run!"

Dr. Sailor came into my room. "The nurses tell me you have a new coping mechanism." He smiled. "May I suggest that to other patients?"

"What do you think about that?" I asked.

"If it ain't broke..." He grinned. "Your resolve is admirable, Anna. Not just to this beat-up old army doc, but to the staff, too. Not to mention a beautiful Austrian woman I know." He winked, and my face reddened at the sweet compliment and the cheeky reference to Hanna.

His reassurance really made me feel good. I also thought it might not be true, but I liked to hear it. I often felt like a demanding, needy patient. Looking back, I know now that I was awful at times, but maybe not as often as I worried about.

"Tomorrow they'll bring the x-ray to your room," Sailor said, nonchalant all of a sudden. "It's a new thing—we need a picture every day."

"Okay," I said. "Why?" It made me afraid.

He pulled up a chair, stared at his fingernails, and then turned his hands down to rest on the tops of his seated legs. Suddenly, our eyes locked.

"Your spinal cord is stuck where the vertebrae

are crushed."

Silence. "Crushed?" I repeated.

He stood up again and put the chair by the wall, turning back to face me.

"Yes—four, five, six, all crushed and dislocated." He seemed to know he was telling me something new.

Lynna started to walk in but picked up on the mood and retreated to the hallway.

"Wow." I gulped. "I didn't know. Shouldn't I have known this before now?" I tried to resist the urge to yell.

"You do need to know," he said softly. "After a week of pictures, I'll meet with the other docs to try to come up with a plan. Meantime, keep meeting with Dr. Bullox—he thinks you're making progress."

The question was, whose progress? Bullox smiled more often, and, with some pushing, he gave up his black suit and started dressing in more flattering colors. I suggested a gym and was surprised he joined; his body took on some form. He started taking an antidepressant. He was one of those clients that "did the work" and improved greatly. His wife decided to stay—he said no!

I rolled my eyes. Sailor started to say more, then thought better of it and left. Lynna came back, just to be there. I was stunned, quiet.

Sam and Glenna decided the plan sounded positive. I grunted, feeling unsure. I was more concerned that these decisions were apparently happening behind my back.

Trusting doctors to decide my life for me, no matter who they were, was not an option.

Visiting hours were almost over when I felt the stagnant air in my room shift just slightly. My daytime companions had already gone home, so I assumed it was one of the staff coming to prod me or poke me or measure me. But I was wrong.

"You," someone snarled. I opened my eyes to see a tall, bulky woman standing at the foot of my bed. The neatness of her coiffed red hair and methodically applied makeup was a strange contrast against the frenzied look on her face. A pair of elegant silver dangling earrings jerked and bobbed against her neck as she gulped in heaving breaths, her body shaking with fury.

"I know this had to be your fault somehow. Maybe you were drunk, maybe you turned in front of him—I don't know! All I know is, you're letting my son take the blame." She was nearly screaming now, her eyes bulging sickeningly out of her face. "That's why you're not suing, isn't it? Because you *know* you did something wrong to land yourself in that bed. Well, maybe I ought to sue you!"

I knew from Mauricio that the boy who'd hit us had lost his father, a firefighter, just a week before the accident. As soon as he filled me in, I'd decided that, so long as I made some sort of recovery, I wouldn't go after the family for money. They'd already suffered enough. But if I stayed paralyzed—a possibility I was still not fully allowing myself to contemplate—I would need some kind of compensation to help me cover the medical bills. And this mother's antagonism was making me reconsider my pledge.

"Well? What do you have to say for yourself, you bitch?" I stared back at her with wide eyes, too shocked to respond.

She was only in my room for a minute or two before a pair of men in black suits stormed in and grabbed her by the arms. They dragged her to the hall, kicking and screaming, and I never heard from her—or her lawyers—again. Later, when I asked one of the nurses where those men had come from, she said they worked for the insurance company. I was assured that from then on, the staff would be more vigilant about unknown visitors.

Though I was still shaken, before long the room settled back into its customary rhythm of beeping and whirring. The evening chugged on, and blissful night descended.

Sleep.

Chapter 7
OCTOBER 1963

As the seasons began to change, my window would catch the bright early sun. The light hit my face just as the day nurse popped into the room with a "Good morning!"

I responded in kind but felt anxious.

"How did you sleep?" she asked.

"Very well. I guess I'm getting accustomed to the constant changes." *Hell, U-turns*, I thought. "Is Lynna off today?"

To be honest, I was annoyed to have another RN. I felt I needed Lynna's calming presence.

She smiled sadly. "She has chemo today. So she is here, but as a patient."

I was stricken. "Why?" A rattle of the bed betrayed my mounting emotion.

"She has cancer. Why else?" The nurse seemed irritated. Maybe she didn't want to talk about it. "I thought you should know."

She moved so she could see my face. I was frightened, but also angry that this woman had confided information that I assumed Lynna wanted to be private. The nurse seemed to enjoy her status of fact provider.

I was still shocked at her news flash. She looked at me closely. "Are you crying? I didn't mean to upset you. You need to toughen up, Miss Anna."

I didn't respond, though I half thought she did intend to distress me. Some of the nurses could be petty about my favoritism toward Lynna. After some idle chatter that I paid little attention to, the nurse turned to leave, and I was alone again with my restless thoughts.

Sam came in early and sat down in his usual place close to the bed, sympathy in his eyes. An hour later, Glenna arrived, and despite my anguish after learning of Lynna's cancer, my mood lifted. Glenna was always so loving and easy, even cheerful. She had a way of boosting those around her. She looked at me in all my special mess and still loved me. Many times, I wished to be more like her—so true, loyal, and giving.

I met Glenna at a gay bar in Los Angeles called the Cork Room. It was that month's place to be. The popular spot always changes, but the people mostly stay the same in gay bars wherever you go. At that time, being gay was chancy, immoral, if not illegal, so they needed patrons to advertise quietly. We all told our group where the "now" places were. As you went from place to place, you acquired favorites, and the Cork Room was one of mine. There was great music, a big dance floor, and, best of all, it was mostly women. Everyone who went in was made to feel included, unlike the places where tight groups would exclude you like they were high school cliques.

It was owned by a woman named Tuck and her lover Alamam. Tuck set strict rules because there could be Vice agents in the gay bars. They came in and joined the frolic, and if anyone offered drugs or sex for money, they would raid. The lights would come on, the music would stop, and everyone would be rudely pushed against the walls. They'd check ID and do searches, and if any violation was found, the bar would close. Tuck's rules kept the Cork Room open.

I'd been in two police raids elsewhere over the years, and the cops were not kind to us in the least. The experience filled me with sadness and an inexplicable sense of inadequacy and shame. Later I met a couple—two men who were both police—and realized people like me were everywhere if you only looked.

When you entered the Cork Room, there was a long stag bar for singles. The rest of the area was a dance floor encircled by cushiony red leather booths. It was clean, well-run, and safe. So was Tuck's other place in Venice Beach. I always felt secure around Tuck; she treated me just a little bit special at a time when I needed that. When you don't have family, the people who step up help you more than they know.

That night, as I sat down with my scotch and soda, I noticed this appealing, very young woman giving me a look. I immediately loved her careful, put together style. She looked honest—open. And she was not shy when she started toward me. *Who is this cute, gutsy woman zeroing in on me?* I thought. She walked across the dance floor and right into my life.

She just came over and said, "Do you dance?" At 23, I had spent years of my life in nightclubs, but I had never gotten up the courage to ask a woman to dance. I said yes.

"Let's see what you've got." She had a very

sensual laugh, and I soon found that she used it a great deal. Most things were funny to her, though never in an unkind way.

We fit nicely, both on the dance floor and in conversation. I was surprised when she said she wanted to come home with me that night. I was with two of my very bored roommates. But they deserved boredom—they usually took me to all-men bars. At six feet tall with short hair, I got groped a lot in those bars. An all-women club was fair game that night. Besides, they had a great time dancing with everyone and enjoying dinner with Tuck, even if they whined about going home alone. Glenna took their silly compliments in stride in her even, secure way. My friends seemed to like her; her presence was soft and pleasant, and she was smart enough to keep up with the jokes.

We left for the 40-minute drive to our place in Pomona, where I worked and attended college. She didn't seem concerned about leaving the bar with three strangers, though I'm not sure I would have chanced it myself. As I got to know her more, it was even more surprising. She was cautious with most new people. I guess we were her exception.

"Nice, you only brought one girl home tonight,"

Mauricio said as we drove. "It's too cold to stand by the gate and take tickets." All of us laughed except Glenna. She didn't say anything, but the gleeful atmosphere turned cool.

"You'll get used to them teasing me, Glenna. It's a constant. Usually funny."

"I'm jealous of my new girlfriend," she confessed. Was she joking? I had only known her about three hours, but something about the way she said it seemed serious. A flashing road sign lit up in my mind.

Glenna, only 19 then, followed me to the backyard by flashlight. By then, she was looking a little apprehensive. The bulk of my furniture was a king-sized mattress on a step-up platform. There was no central heat, very little light, and a coffee can to pee in. Someone had just given me a chair.

Glenna tried in vain to lock the door. "It's never locked." I smiled. She did not return it. The chicken coop was clean, fancy even, but still recognizable for what it was. I tried to assure her she was safe. She tried to look assured.

I went to bed, and she sat up in my only chair. At one point, I woke up and saw that she was on the edge of the mattress, shivering. I sat straight up, scooped her slight body into my arms, and put her under the electric blanket, thinking she was cold. She was so frightened that she stayed there the rest of the night, eyes wide open.

I slept as I always do, slumbering like a baby until 6 a.m. when I pop right up into a new day. Glenna was exactly where I left her, under the blanket but still uneasy. "Why did you come with us?" I asked.

She sat up, chin quivering. "I thought you were a regular person. You know, living in a house. Nothing like this!"

The morning light made my place more friendly. Mauricio brought us coffee and Mexican sweet bread. It was warm and sunny outside, and we moved to my tiny, sweet patio with two chairs. She started to relax. "No sex last night?" she joked, a coy look in her eyes. I smiled. I liked this girl. She was certainly going to keep me on my toes.

We never separated after that night, and Glenna became my first live-in lover. We spent the time to really know one another. Until then, I'd had many women friends, usually married, and we kept it easy—no real connection. I'd liked the ease of living alone with friends, and I never wanted to play house. If I had wanted that, marriage to a man would have been an easier life. Sometimes I wondered if I could have both—the freedom and the intimacy—with a gay woman. Unlikely.

This girl was younger, and I was ready to try a real relationship. I'd been on my own since I was 17, and Glenna offered me many wonderful things. One of those was a close, loving family. I had none. Hers didn't exactly know what our connection was, but if their daughter was happy, they were happy. Her parents, Hector and Edith, were loving and unpretentious. Tribal members of the Choctaw Nation, they had moved from Oklahoma to California in search of "the good life."

It was a very sweet time that taught me many needed, life-affirming lessons. Glenna stuck it out with me through thick and thin. But I had no concept of monogamy, and I explained that to her. She kept thinking I would change because she was devoted to me. Despite the list of expectations we had drawn up, she still thought that if I cared for her enough, I would "be true to her."

She was wrong. I knew it hurt her, caused her so much sadness. I always felt some guilt, but never enough. The way I saw it, I always was true to her, except for a few purely sexual interests.

In my mind, if I wanted to be married, I could have been on three different occasions. I wanted to be gay. To me, that must mean no attachment, just love until it ends—and it always does, in my never-to-be-humble opinion. Changing my philosophy to believe in one person for life was never my intent. It might have been my unusual upbringing, but to me, committing to only one person long-term was, for most people, a lie. In the back of my mind, a vague plan formed. Maybe at around 60 years old I would settle down and become that true, monogamous person until the end. Who knew if I could really do it?

Glenna's jealousy wasn't lying to her, but she had a bad side within her, and it made us both miserable often. She rarely drank, but when she did, all bets were off. Once, she took my keys and hid my car while I was at a bar with a friend, Flo, whom she suspected of being more than a friend. Then she stormed into the joint and confronted me, chasing me around the pool table with a cue stick. When we finally found the car and made our way home, she was waiting there, dead drunk, to demand that I leave. Eventually, she ran out into the yard without her clothes on, and I had to tackle her to the ground and drag her back inside.

She hadn't been wrong about Flo. But her outbursts weren't always warranted.

The bottom line was that I had told her where I stood that very first morning. The following years were full of love, disappointment, anger, trust, suspicion, sex—the usual ingredients of life.

As I looked at her in my hospital room, sitting on the window bench bathed in sunlight, I felt so much love for her. And that never caused me significant guilt about the other people. It's sad, but true. I smiled. *Now she knows what I'm doing every moment,* I thought. *Wonder if that's any better for her?*

In a way, it's what she always wanted. For her, the worst period of my life just might have been a relief. Even in that place and time, I still had to smile about Radcliff. I really was "a bit of a jerk."

That day seemed more boring than usual. Then the three of us perked up as the timbre of the noise in the hallway seemed to change. Our attention turned toward the door and Mauricio, Kip, Robin, and Billy marched into the room.

Loud taped burlesque music filled the space—ba-ba-ba-bom-bom! They had cloths wrapped around their heads, T-shirts tied in knots in the front, makeshift toilet paper eyelashes on their lids, and bright red paint on their lips. They did this bump and grind dance around the room as two of the nurses marched along banging in time on stainless steel bedpans. The noise was deafening. We all howled with glee. It must have gone on for only a few moments, but it brightened the whole day.

Looking back, I realize how inappropriate this must have seemed to the other patients. As outrageous as it was, we adored the constant push toward life, toward fun. I loved these men as my brothers, my family. That day's delight was a thermos of margaritas and a set of tiny paper cups. Everyone except me imbibed a little. As they sipped, we heard the speaker above my bed click off.

These young, sweet men never stopped trying to cheer my lot. About once a week, they would think up something to entertain us—reading aloud dramatically from a favorite book, bringing a special food. They were so generous in every way. At times—many times—they kept me alive. But late at night, I thought about how it couldn't last. Someday their fortitude would fail, and I would be in that bed alone. But until then, I would cherish each outlandish moment.

The hospital staff let it happen, even enjoyed the spectacle. I felt my sad circumstance brought understanding and even acceptance for people like us. I really don't think they forgot us quickly. I hoped they didn't assign us to a category of "the good queers"—that they realized their gay uncle was not some anomaly. Maybe now they could be that much more open and accepting for their gay daughter or son. Their wife or husband, their boss, their teacher. Their nurse.

Maybe it helped them realize that people like us were doing great work everywhere.

There was one afternoon nurse who was upset about the day they brought music and slow danced with each other, man to man, but she was quieted by her nurse friends. All of the commotion helped me stay grateful, and that gratitude was a saving grace for me; I never expected these people who stuck with me to do all they did to keep me going. Whenever I felt overwhelmed or defeated, I would remember they expected better of me. I would clear my mind and adjust the invisible crown they had saddled me with.

I gladly accepted the responsibility, but the other feelings—the anxiety, the uncertainty—were not far behind.

I couldn't get complacent. I had to stay stiff about getting out of this bed. I couldn't give in to acceptance.

After my usual morning chores—eat, clean up, change sheets, x-ray, take blood, change catheter, enema, exercises, lotion, inspect for bed sores, and on and on and on—the nurses would fill me in on the hospital gossip. The talk enchanted me and relaxed me until it was time for my meditation escape. The last person lingering seemed to understand and usually wished me a happy trip. It's amazing how your mind can stifle you or free you.

That day I had talked a little about my childhood. They were curious about the lack of family visitors, and they'd find any way to approach the question. As I lay there, I thought about my grandma, who everyone called Babe. She was my champion—a businesswoman who liked to dress up and went to work every day, seven days a week, at 4 p.m. She never drove; her driver, Jake, always took her to work in a shiny black two-year-old car.

I couldn't remember a time Jake wasn't there. People would say she dressed him up "like her pet monkey." I was too young then to fully comprehend the racism lurking behind the jeer. But I saw Jake as an uncle and protector. He was always patient with me, a very precocious child who was seemingly trying for most adults.

After Babe's husband died in a car accident, his lawyer friends set her up in business: a brothel. She ran a clean, responsible house. Women came from the local colleges, where they were working on degrees with little income to support them. She fixed that.

Jake stayed at the house, which was called Sixth Street, and we also had a private doctor, Dr. Mitchner. I lived in a separate home with Babe, but I loved to visit the many rooms of Sixth Street. I spent most of my time in a private area on the third floor, a circular apartment with windows all around it that looked straight into the trees. Some of the women lived in the building, but those with children were housed in apartments around town. They were allowed ample time for school and study. I loved when the women would stop to talk with me.

My father was Babe's son and youngest child. He was a bright, handsome young man before he was drafted to the army, along with two of his neighbor friends, at 20 years old. My father was on the first Allied team of photographers sent into Auschwitz prison camp after World War II. Then he disappeared, and our family was notified he was missing in action. The Red Cross later found him in France in a mental hospital. He was sent home, but he never recovered.

He was violent, and very ill, and would spend most of his life at Winter VA Hospital in Topeka. He called it the country club. His daily routine was up at 7 a.m., gym, breakfast, nap, lunch, swim, group or counseling, nap, dinner, and then a dance or other entertainment. He called the co-ed dances bush therapy—apparently, there was lots of sex.

When I was 12 years old, Babe gave me a two-year-old car so I could go get my dad for the weekend pass visits she arranged. (We never bought new, because we couldn't show we had money.) During his time out of the hospital he drank, used drugs, and created an alarming variety of awful situations all around him. He beat me; he molested my younger sister. He made life horrible for my grandmother and his two siblings.

When he was "out," our family was on frightened high alert. My aunt and her daughter would sit in a central bathroom with no windows. They did not answer their phone or the door. Uncle Norman, my father's brother, always sat in the dark and went to bed early.

Thanks to my father, I have eye damage for life. He gave me several concussions and seven broken ribs, and he cracked most of my teeth. Our Sixth Street doctor would come stay with me until I recovered, so there were no official reports. He hated my dad and tried to get Babe to leave him in the hospital. But her answer was always no.

"He just needs some home cooking, the love of

family," she would say. "He'll get himself back and be okay." He never did. She said he was a wounded World War II hero, and she had to help. Her son simply could not be locked away for answering his country's call to serve.

On my 17th birthday, he came after me, and my Grandma Babe tried to protect me. He killed her right before my eyes. Then he was hospitalized. He died there at 42 years old. Not a day too soon, in my opinion.

"Anna. Anna, are you okay?" It was Glenna. "You seem distressed—are you sick?"

Her voice pulled me from my memories. I never told her about this part of my story; compared to her family, we were insane. It was a source of shame for me. People that became aware of our family history often treated me differently, my mother's side of the family included. They would not speak to or of Grandma Babe, even after she died.

It took me a moment to get back to reality. "Oh. Just a bad trip," I said as I emerged into the hospital room. For once, I was happy to be there. Despite the cast obscuring my body, I felt exposed; uncomfortable.

"What was that about?" she asked, looking down at me with soft, loving eyes. She reached out to take my hand but then remembered my aversion and pulled it back.

"Just not being able to be free. Feeling trapped." I paused. "I know you understand. You must feel it, too, sitting in this room every day."

She nodded. "I sit and watch you every day. What you're able to get through is amazing. I don't know how you do it."

"It helps not to feel alone. But what choice do I have, Glenna? What choice?" Now I was becoming dismayed again. "It was nothing—just sort of a bad dream."

I had never told anyone how Grandma Babe died. She was the kind of person who had always been bursting with life, and I was looking right at her at the moment her eyes lost the light that had always been there. I can still see them. I was the last thing she could comprehend. I wish to this day that I had stayed out of the house that night. I could have found a quiet country road and slept in my car as I had so many other nights when Dad was out. But that time I went home, and my life changed forever.

That was when I moved to California in 1956 and stayed with my mother for about a month. She just never could deal with me. Then I was on my own—thank God! I never looked back, and my mother's family never looked for me. When they were made aware of my romantic preferences, I think they felt vindicated. After all, I was raised by "that whore."

It took me several days to put those memories back in the past. From then on, I was careful to start my journey with good thoughts on my out-of-room trips into the depths of my mind.

But inside of that hospital room and out, my grandmother has always been with me. She loved me, pushed my education, accepted who I was as a young kid. I was so fortunate to have had a woman so brilliant in my life.

I will always regret that we parted so early and so violently.

Chapter 8
NOVEMBER 1963

I tried not to focus on that demon ceiling tile. The bed was tilted up at the head so I could see through my window, and things outside were moving along. It was sunny and green out. I could see the cars in the parking lot—so many colors.

I thought about the first car that I purchased with my own savings. It was fire engine red and even had a red interior—a 1959 Ford Galaxy, paid for with $3,211.20 in cash. Sadly, it never ran. I got a loan on it, then took it to the back parking lot of the dealership and abandoned it with a detailed note about the problems. The motor was too big for the radiator, and Ford would not help me. The bank had an attorney I hoped would be more able to do something about it, but there were no lemon laws at that time. Instead, I used the loan money to get a used car that worked. To this day, I'm very careful about anything I purchase. It was a hard lesson well learned.

The day nurse came in and, strangely, announced herself. I thought she looked distressed but let it pass. She stayed in the room but didn't make the usual chatter. It made me anxious.

"What's up?" I inquired. She pretended she didn't hear me. *Oh no*, I thought. *Now what?* The x-ray people shuffled in to take their second picture of the day. It felt like the quiet calm before a Kansas storm.

Then Dr. Waters and Dr. Sailor walked into the room. "You guys are scaring me," I said. "Get on with it." I noticed Sailor was dressed in a suit and tie. He cleaned up well. "You look very nice today," I offered, wondering if he was seeing Hanna for lunch. I was always grasping at straws about their relationship. I liked putting the details together, real or imagined. It was none of my business, but it did keep me entertained.

"We need to discuss a few things with you today," Waters started, taking his seat close to my bed. They must have organized a dress code.

Waters was also wearing a suit—blue was really his color—and a plaid tie finished the look.

Sailor stood at my feet. "We now feel certain your spinal cord is severed, and it cannot be repaired." As he spoke, Sailor's eyes were fixed on the bed, not on me. I felt like a large bug that had just hit the windshield of a very fast-moving truck.

"We are suggesting surgery to stabilize your vertebrae to prevent more damage," said Dr. Waters. "You're still breathing on your own, but our concern is that, due to the crushed bone in your neck, that could stop. We are trying to keep you from living on a ventilator for life."

I opened my mouth. Nothing came out.

At this point, my brain was trying to make an exit through my ear. "What is the surgery? Will it improve anything?"

"We don't expect any significant improvement. This would be to prevent more complications," said Waters. "We would put two pins vertically in your spine so it can't further reduce the separation you still have. We now think this is the best next step."

Both men had stopped eye contact. The room was still, save for the repetitive sounds that emanated from various pieces of equipment.

"You both agree?" I asked, looking from man

to man. I felt my hope fizzling.

"Yes, we do."

"If you're right, I won't improve." Anger was starting to win out in the ugly war of my emotions.

"Yes, that is our opinion."

"So you're here today, all dressed up, to tell me my life is over."

No one offered anything more. I sought out my trusty ceiling tile.

The nurse was still in the room; she had moved to my side. Dr. Sailor had tears in his eyes.

"This makes you sad, does it, Doctor?" I sneered.

He just stood there. "We just don't have the resources needed to fix this, Anna. We are so sorry." His voice was quiet. "It's okay to be angry right now."

"Can I think about this?"

"Yes, but not for long. Time is important with this."

My eyes locked on the window. I refused to participate in any more conversation. The devastation was too much. Somehow, I had thought I was getting better. I had been wrong.

I longed for my cozy cave out of reach of this life I was being dragged through. Though I had never felt so sad, so helpless, I couldn't bring myself to cry. I pushed my mind back to the car lot. I wanted to take off and drive as fast as I could to the mountains, windows open, wind in my hair. *I will never feel that exhilaration again,* I thought. *Why couldn't I have died in the accident?*

I needed someone, something to blame, but I came up empty.

I'm not sure when they left my room, but then it was 7 p.m. and Radcliff was there. She seemed to know to be quiet. People came into the room and left again without a word. No one talked—I just couldn't. The night passed with no sleep.

The ceiling tile was somehow a comfort.

I was startled from my stupor at 7 a.m. "Sorry I was off yesterday," Lynna said. "How are you?"

She stood by the bed ready to hear my version of what she'd surely already read in my chart.

"How the fuck do you think I am, Lynna? Just dandy, thanks. You want to help me walk out of here?"

"Angry I see," she replied. "That's good." She patted my forehead as I dissolved into sobs like a disappointed child.

"What the hell are you talking about?" I asked,

peering at her serious face, trying to discern whether that was hope I saw behind her eyes. Could Lynna really say something to pull me back from the brink once again?

"I know what you were told yesterday," she confessed. "What do you think you'll do?" She rolled up a chair, sat down, and looked at me expectantly.

I stared at her, amazed. "Oh, do I have a decision to make? I'm going to be a quad. The good news is, maybe I'll be able to breathe. Then again, maybe not!"

The waterworks turned on again. It felt good to cry about it, out loud, without holding back. She got a towel and wiped my face.

She usually never sat down, but she took a seat again beside my bed. "I'm not supposed to interfere, but if it costs me my job, you're worth it. You've just come so far."

I perked up. "What do you know?" I asked hopefully. My bed shook and rattled as I trembled wildly, trying to focus. What was she suggesting? "God, Lynna, I feel a hundred years old!"

"That's the thing," she said. "The doctors don't actually know any more than you or I do about what might happen. What's the rush? You were told the same thing by McDaniel, and he didn't get the time of day from you. So why are you willing to give up so easily now?"

She went on, "Nothing has really changed. So, take your time. You're stable in this bed, in traction, in that cast. These men seem to want to move this along, but you don't have to let them." She looked at me, smiling. "Just take your time, please. I have a good feeling about you, and waiting won't make it more dangerous than it already is. If you can't breathe, we can handle that, too. God knows we have before."

My breathing slowed as her words began to sink in. In that instant, it felt as though life was suddenly switched on again. She was right. Stop the rush—it's my life! Lynna stuck her head back in the door as she left. "Just don't fire anyone else." She giggled, disappearing.

The next day, I asked to see Dr. Sailor. He came by around noon and stood by my bed as though I had a gun. It did mean something to me that he felt so badly. Maybe it made me feel less alone in all of this mess.

"I'm not having the surgery yet," I said decidedly, ready to defend my position.

To my surprise, he looked relieved. "Okay, I'll tell Dr. Waters." His eyes sort of twinkled. "I have another option for you. Your cast is not working as we hoped, so we need to take it off and redo the way it's set at the site of your injury."

It was like whiplash. They weren't trying to talk me into their surgery? Instead, they were handing me another awful proposal. *God, take me now.*

"Oh no," I said, already beginning to cry. "The first time nearly killed me."

"We did not nearly kill you, Anna," he said, a touch of pride coloring his voice. "I do admit it was a little too primitive. We can and will do better in the operating room." He touched my cheek. "This will be really hard, I know, but it's our best chance." *A chance at what, exactly?* I thought. He didn't say, and I certainly didn't ask.

"You're a fighter, and I'm counting on that." He turned to leave the room. "Tomorrow morning."

It was too fast—right out the frying pan and into the fire. I wondered when they had made all these decisions without my knowledge.

"Don't forget to shave my head!" If I had to endure this again, I was at least going to get some kind of relief from it.

"Got it," he said over his shoulder, smiling.

A little while later, another voice broke into my thoughts.

"So? How are you?" It was Lynna.

"Better," I said. She looked tired. *Funny,*

I thought. *I know so little about her life, and here she is hip deep in mine.*

"One thing, Lynna."

"Yes?"

"I would like to think that one day, after all this is over, you and I could meet for lunch. That we could stay friends. You've helped me so much."

She held my eyes. "Yes," she agreed. "We definitely will."

"You're scheduled for the operating room for your cast at 6 a.m.," she went on. "I'm so proud of you, Anna. He's a genius who loves a challenge. You're in good hands."

"Could you be there tomorrow?" I asked. "Please try."

"Yes," she answered, "already approved by Dr. Sailor and Dr. Waters."

Relief filled my soul.

My Pomona boys arrived later that evening, all clothed in black dresses, armed with silly eulogies and dead flowers. They were throwing me a wake and, despite my dismay about what I would endure the following day, I loved the idea.

Kip had prepared a tongue-in-cheek tribute to my life so far. "Was she an honorable person?"

"Hell no!" my friends gleefully shouted back in unison.

"And did she live her life well?"

"No, she lived her life medium rare!" Robin offered.

"And was she nice to her friends?"

"No, she was a real bitch most of the time!" Billy called, a grin nearly splitting his face in two.

I couldn't help but laugh. When my boys were around, even the darkest moments became flooded with sunlight.

That night I just couldn't get to sleep. Things felt so tight, constricting, cramped. I was wild with anticipation, deeply edged with fear. I could see the clock and at about 1:30 a.m. I realized someone was in the room, sitting in the dark. The soft whoosh of their breathing was just audible in the silent blackness.

"Who are you?" I whispered. I wouldn't have been surprised if they'd answered, "I am an angel of death, here to collect you." I wasn't fearful, but it was a first for this kind of thing.

"It's Dr. Waters, Anna." He stayed in his seat, his soft, low voice filling the still, dark space. He just paused then, quiet. I knew he lived miles away. Why was he sitting in my room? I felt uneasy. Surprises had been bountiful over the past few days. I was sensitive to any slight change, and this did not seem slight.

"Is something wrong?" I asked, my voice now squeaky with fear.

"No, no," he said quickly. "I just thought you might be worried tonight and might like some support. I wanted you to know we're all doing our best for you. We're trying everything we know how to." His voice sounded tense. I felt more afraid. Confused, I just stayed still and waited for the other shoe to drop.

The damn bed shook again. It always gave away my anger or fear. There were no hidden feelings here. In my position, everything seemed to hang out in the open—everything.

"Do you have questions about tomorrow?" His voice was light, sweet—positive. It was just a little too professional, too tightly controlled. But I felt the concern behind his control. It cooled my uneasy mind, though only slightly.

"I don't really understand why it's needed," I admitted. "Why change the cast? It's so hot when it's new and I'm really not looking forward to that." A loud sob escaped from my body. "My last casting experience was awful, you know that."

He didn't speak for a moment. I tried to let the calming darkness of the room seep in. *Breathe*, I told myself.

"Your neck isn't positioned well enough to release the tension on your spinal cord. We're going to try again, hoping for a better result. I won't lie, you'll be in extreme pain—it will be tough, but I believe it's worth a try." He walked to the bedside. The fatigue in his eyes was evident. He looked so different in that hooded sweatshirt, its red color almost glowing in the dim light. He seemed taller than I noticed before.

Despite his tiredness, I could feel how sure of himself he was. His posture was strong. He always seemed certain he was in the right place, doing the right thing. Confidence personified.

As he leaned down to kiss my cheek, I breathed in his scent. He always smelled like he had just stepped out of a shower, like good soap. He quickly turned toward the door. "I heard you want your head shaved." He laughed. "We usually think it's traumatic for ladies to have their long hair cut off."

"Not me." I grinned. "It's crawling inside the cast. I can't wait."

We both laughed. "See you at 6 a.m."

"Okay. Thanks, Dr. Waters. I think I can sleep now."

He was gone, and a few moments later, the night nurse came in. "What was that?" she asked, smiling. "I've never had a doctor do that ever. He's a special one." I stayed quiet. She knew I agreed. It made me feel important; lucky.

"He prescribed a sleeping shot for you, too. You need to rest—tomorrow is a big day."

The drugs did their work.

I was so warm as I slept that I could even feel my neck relax.

It seemed like only a few seconds before Lynna was by my bed. "Good morning! It's 4 a.m. We need to get you ready for the recasting," she said. We did all the usual, enema (*Good idea,* I thought), catheter, bath, oxygen. We raised the head of my bed to almost perpendicular, to get me accustomed to sitting up. The room went into a tailspin—how long had it been since I was upright?

I had a strap around my chest under my arms to

hold me up. It felt good, until I suddenly vomited on the plastic sheet Lynna had tucked in front of me—which is not easy with a cast around your head. "Good job!" She cheered, wrapping up the plastic and putting it in a bin.

"Did you know I would do that?"

"Why yes, I did." She laughed.

She flopped into the chair by my bed. "Now we wait. They said no food or water this morning." By now it was 5:30 a.m. and Julian was there to attach my oxygen and check that my traction was in place.

"Because it's attached to your head," he said. "Don't want it to get stuck someplace." We laughed.

Soon we were in the surgical area. "We need to change her clothes," Lynna joked, gesturing to my cast. Julian wished me luck and left.

Now it was getting real. Lynna stayed all business, her eyes down as I was pushed into the operating room. It looked different this time; all shiny and surgical. Much closer to what I imagined an OR should look like. It was that same room with that same big window, except this time the window was dark. It felt more private.

"No audience today?" I asked. "Did we fail our audition last time?" A sheepish laugh circulated, then the room quieted.

"Our reviews were really bad," said Sailor.

I was sitting up in my CircOlectric bed, with the back part removed. That was Dr. Sailor's place. Waters had the x-ray machine at my right side, Lynna was on my left, and the traction was in its usual spot on the bed—no light fixture attachment, no stool with rollers.

"This is more like it!" I said. They all agreed. "Though it does dampen the excitement a bit." Silently, I wondered if we were here again today due to the fiasco of last time. I couldn't have been the only one with the question in my mind.

The smell of the warm, wet plaster tape wafting toward me made me want to run. *No chance of that,* I mused. This was not for the faint of heart.

Dr. Sailor's face was pink under his surgical mask. They placed a mirror in front of me so I could see the show. "I know you don't like to miss anything," Dr. Sailor said. He leaned down to my ear and whispered, "Hanna told me." I was surprised he would say that, but I was delighted. I had been kept at arm's length with their affair, and I appreciated the glimpse into his personal life. She was more careful with his reputation—very tight-lipped.

"Ready, A?" Dr. Waters said.

"Yes," I replied. "Fingers crossed."

"Let's go." We all took an audible deep breath.

They removed my blankets, so I was nude from the cast down. "We need to saw you out from the top of your shoulder," Sailor said.

"So why does my twizzy need to be uncovered?"

He laughed. "I need to be sure you can sit in this cast when I'm done. We'll measure the length to be sure."

Lynna placed a privacy towel over my lap.

"Thank you."

"The saw is surgical," Waters added. "So if it touches flesh, it stops. It can't cut you." I relaxed.

"It's noisy," Lynna said. It was right next to my ears. But within what seemed like only a few moments, my head was free.

"I thought it would feel good," I shouted over the din. "It doesn't!"

"You're accustomed to the protection and the warmth. Everything is going as it should be," Dr. Waters said.

"We'll get you cleaned up," Lynna said as she came forward. "Then it will really feel good." She used some special soap to scrub my neck and shoulders. Then they started setting up to cut my hair.

A surgical nurse took Sailor's place. "Wow," she said. "There's still gravel and blood from the accident in her hair." I heard a pair of clippers make a welcome buzz. For a moment, it reminded me of the BUZZ that had filled my head in those first chaotic days. "Your hair is long," the nurse said hesitantly. My head was itchy, and to make matters worse, there was plaster dust everywhere, even with the vacuum on the saw. I wanted it all gone.

"Just take it off! I'm tired of all the hair crap. It's a constant problem, and I can't wait to get rid of it. It smells awful." Everyone grunted in agreement. Humiliating as these situations are, no one can afford to spare your feelings. "Please just get this over with."

"Her hair has been a constant struggle, crawling under that cast," Lynna chimed in. "Anna is not a problem patient. It's a hard day, and the hair is the bonus."

The two nurses gave me a knowing look in my mirror. "You'll feel better now," the one with the clippers said.

Then my hair was past tense. "Oh, thank you. Thank you."

"I'll put it in a bag for you—it'll be in your room."

I wonder why, I thought as Lynna and I made eye contact. We just shrugged. She really had a knack for being on the same page with me. Surely my hair, still stiff with blood, dirt, and gravel, wouldn't be considered something of value?

Someone reminded me again how "most women" reacted to losing their hair. It made me livid. Had they talked to many women recently?

Dr. Sailor was ready to put a new gauze sock over my head. "We're releasing your traction for a few moments," he told me. "This is Dr. Vise. She is a respiratory specialist, in case your breathing stops."

"My what?" I said, surprised.

Before I knew it, the traction was taken from the overhead support and everything else released, too.

My breathing did stop as Sailor quickly slipped the sock over my head and the traction was reattached. I was a slab of bacon, no thought, no feeling, and no breath. In this new life, everything came as a surprise, and I was beginning to think I didn't like surprises.

Dr. Vise pushed into my throat, and her little machine gave a big gush of oxygen. The room relaxed.

"Well done, Doctor!" *Ho ho ho*. The compliment angered me for a moment. But the warm, damp, head-to-hip plaster was complete. They all agreed it looked much better and there were congrats all around. I was wheeled back down the hall, bed and all, and parked in my room. It was 1 p.m.

Dr. Waters was there. "We'll increase your traction now, so you may feel some discomfort," he said. Beginning to understand the code, I braced myself for my next surprise.

"Okay, I guess," I said as I began to drift to sleep, exhausted. Dr. Vise was in the doorway.

"Should I intubate her?" she asked.

"No, wait," Waters said. "See how she does."

These conversations about me always made me feel like a rumpled, forgotten basket of clothes. Hot or cold water? Bleach or no bleach? How much soap? All decisions were made for me, casually, and right in front of me. It actually made me laugh. *I wonder if this will be my life from this point.* Not if I had anything to do with it. I looked at my silly ceiling tile.

This has to work.

Chapter 9

The pain came on in spurts and stops until it was intolerable. I screamed, maybe all day and into the night. Never have I ever felt such agony.

Radcliff was there, and she told me they were resetting my neck—rebreaking it. There was no other way to do it. "No," I begged. "Something is wrong."

Everything was a blur as they increased my traction and pulled my neck back into a taut line. Radcliff tried to say or do something to comfort me, but nothing could touch this indescribable pain.

"You just have to see it through," she said.

"I'll stay tonight in case you need me. I'll be right here for you."

Dr. Waters was called. He said it was expected, it was alright, and he was unsure how long it would take. He said he would stay in the hospital all night if I needed him. They changed my sheets several times; they were soaked with sweat. It seemed to me it should have been blood.

At 1 a.m., Radcliff went home. Later that night—I have no idea what time—a nurse stood by my bed, her hand on my forehead, reassuring me everything would be okay. She eventually lay down next to me, wiping the sweat from my face, telling me over and over not to worry and that I'd be alright. *Breathe into your pain.* It was wonderful not to be alone, to have someone next to me offering encouraging words all night.

Lynna roused me at about 9 a.m. "Can you wake up, or should I leave you sleeping?"

No answer came to me as she took my vitals and started to set up my bath. "Who stayed with me last night? I want to thank them."

"What are you asking?" she said, and I explained.

"No one would do that, Anna. They would be punished for that," Lynna said.

"It happened!" I insisted. "Why would they be in trouble? It helped!"

"No—you must have been delusional from the pain. Your blood pressure is way too high. I'll call Dr. Sailor."

No matter what they told me, I knew she had been there. It might have been my angel, but I will never be convinced I was alone.

Lynna paused. "You're Catholic, right? Would a priest make things easier? It might help you."

"Am I dying, Lynna? If so, please just be straight with me."

"As I understand it," she said slowly, "last rites can either help you heal, or prepare you for a peaceful death."

"Okay," I agreed.

Suddenly, Dr. Sailor was in my room. My head felt like an overinflated balloon. I searched for any sign of a smile, but there was none.

"You look awful," I said.

"Gee, thanks."

"Am I dying?" I asked again. He didn't say no. *All that hard-earned education*, I thought. *So hard won, and I'll never get to use it.*

Then Father French entered the room. I knew him from when I lived in Pomona, though I had long since been shunned from his parish on Holt Avenue.

"Hello, Anna. You've asked for the sacrament?" He didn't seem to recognize me. Either that, or he was choosing to ignore our history.

"Yes, Father." I looked at him in disbelief, not sure what to say next. "This will help me either way, is that right?"

He said yes. "It will help you die in grace, or it will help you regain your health."

He completed his part, I completed mine. My pain was so harsh that I screamed several times. Now I was blessed and prepared for my demise. I felt no fear, just lightning bolts of searing pain. We waited to see what would happen next.

Lynna stayed with me, and Glenna was there, but no one else was allowed in. I think I was sedated, because I woke up the next day, day three since the reset of my neck. I was alone and the sun was bright, very peaceful. *Am I dead?* I wondered.

Someone dropped a metal bedpan in the hallway. *Nope—still here.*

After my cast was repositioned, time moved very slowly. Routine set in as a now irreversible fact of my life. All involved were kind and patient, but it was not a period of time that I could tolerate. I tried to be pleasant, but my demeanor was always tinged with fear and anger. My life, in my mind, was not acceptable. I was finally defeated.

The pain was all-consuming. Though I still couldn't feel my body or move my limbs, it was somehow everywhere, like hot oil poured with excruciating slowness. Sometimes the bursts of fire would last no more than five minutes, but other times I would go on burning for hours, trapped in the flame like kindling. I couldn't get away from it. I couldn't breathe through it. I was forced to sit there and let it incinerate me to ash.

Miserable was the word for the month of November. I had made occasional efforts to live this disconnected life, just to tumble right back down to the bottom of the hill where I began. I could no longer muster the strength to try. My escapes into meditation helped, but I never wanted to return to that hospital bed. No one—not my friends, the nursing staff, the doctors—could reach me. I was lost. Suicidal. Desperate.

The days came and went with little notice from me. I had become microscopic—reduced to a tiny prick of light in a vast sea of darkness. I retreated into myself, struggling to see the point of talking, of eating, of being aware. The walls leaned in like the bars of a cell, and I gave myself over to total despair. I was trapped in an overwhelming cloud of nothingness.

Nothing but the hurt.

In mid-November I had a bedsore on my heel, and they were all upset to see that I couldn't have cared less. Then I noticed they must have done something to my foot when they were treating it—it was burning. Had they left something on my skin? There I was, my foot in flames, unable to move. I yelled to the intercom for help. I'd never done that before.

Lynna and two other nurses were suddenly at my feet. Holding my right foot and moving it around, Lynna said, "Nothing's wrong. It looks okay."

"But it's not okay," I said, "it's on fire!" I screamed, and they rushed to close my door.

They all looked at each other as I waited for help. Then they all looked at me and their expressions changed. "You're feeling localized pain!"

All talking over each other, they repeated, "Are you feeling pain in your foot?" We were all in different states of disbelief.

"Are you sure that's what's happening?" I asked. Tears streamed down all of our faces.

"Yes! You're feeling your foot! That's proof the pain is worth it." They ran out into the hall. "Call Sailor and Waters, Anna can feel her foot!"

Over the next few days, that life-giving, scorching sensation crept over my entire body. I had never been in so much extreme pain, nor had I ever been so exhilarated by so much hurt. It felt like I was being dipped in hot french fry grease. Would I stay like this? Dr. Waters could not answer that question.

He said Sailor's recasting had worked, but to what extent, no one could tell. For me, it was a confusing time, one of euphoria tinged with fear. I could not sleep, and food was difficult to keep down. The right side of my body had some feeling, and I could move my arm, which was both bad and good. It would get signals that I didn't send and at times surge up without warning and hit me in the face. Those working to help me at times had to duck to avoid being hit. They would laugh and accuse me of intentional strikes.

Gratefully, they all found it funny. Everyone was a bit emotional. Dr. Sailor actually stood in my room and sobbed. That upset me; it made me aware that I still could lose it all. He said he really hoped, but doubted, that his efforts would be successful. But it was working. My recovery and my future were not set, but all bets were now better odds. Lynna was very smug and silly about being so right. If she had not said to wait, who knows? But she did, and I listened.

If you could fully embody love, respect, and gratitude in one person, she was it for me. Was this what she did for all of her patients? In some selfish way, I wanted her skill, her caring to be just for me. But I felt sure she was the same consummate professional with all of her patients.

I found it more difficult to celebrate. My pain was still white hot, even though it was less constant now. It was all I could tolerate, at times more. It was as though my wide-angle world was shrinking to a pinpoint. I couldn't scream or cry. At the same time, I felt guilty. My lot had changed from feeling nothing to putting my body on a hot stove. That was progress, and I should be grateful. But not being able to jump back, I just cooked. I was always waiting for the next shoe to drop.

Someone mentioned that laughter helped pain. Soon, most people tried to help by being funny, offering a joke. One of my favorites was: "Why are turds tapered? To keep your ass from slamming shut." That, for some reason, hit my funny bone.

But it could only help so much.

As this went on and on, day after day, I couldn't talk, eat, or care about my surroundings. The pain took all my attention and energy. I thought again about people who simply combust into ash. If this was to be my cure, no thank you—I wanted out. If the kind staff tried to move me or change anything, the pain of their touch was excruciating. Even the sheet that covered me caused me pain. Cold water felt hot. It seemed every nerve in my body was getting that same message.

The pain might have been worse than losing feeling. While my caregivers celebrated, I became more desperate.

Then one late November morning, Lynna was trying to talk me into a cool bath. But cold water hurt, too. "No!" I answered. "Please!"

I saw Lynna's patient but exasperated expression and started crying. "You were able to sleep last night?" she queried.

"I did," I said, finally engaged but looking like a frightened rabbit.

"Are you in less pain?" she asked. I diverted

my eyes, knowing what she wanted to hear. For the first time in seemingly weeks, I looked out the window. *It's almost winter,* I realized. *When did that happen?*

"Only if you don't touch me. Please, Lynna, everything hurts. Can you just skip the routine today? Please?" Now I was begging.

She moved closer to the face opening in my cast. Looking like a proud mother, she said, "I've had a hold of your right foot since I came into the room, and you didn't even notice." I looked down, surprised.

"Your pain is letting go. Your spinal cord is being released. You're expecting extreme pain, but it's lessening. You need to wake yourself up and realize how goddamn lucky you are right at this moment." By now, she was almost shouting.

"Are you sure, Lynna?" I asked with hesitation. "Are you sure?"

"Have I ever lied to you? Wake up." She seemed to glow, and it was catching. "You've been in so much pain that you expect it. Give in to being better. Let go."

"Is my leg moving?"

"No. But your foot did." She grinned. "By God, Anna, you were right. You are going to get out of that damn bed and walk away." Then she caught herself. "Hopefully."

I looked around the room, feeling more awake but still unsure. I felt a grand sadness, intensely afraid of being wrong again. I wept for a long time. Maybe I would never regain my old sense of surety, of clarity, of protection. Maybe this had changed me so much that I would be fearful now for the rest of my life. The ache of uncertainty was devastating.

But when did I accept that I would be a quad? When did I lose confidence in the doctors and in Lynna? I was embarrassed, but I was on my way back. This body of mine kept the faith when my cautious spirit failed. I could see now that though it hurt when my right arm flew up to hit me in the eye, it was also tangible progress.

At 7 p.m. that night, I kept looking at the doorway. I was rewarded when Radcliff strutted into my room. She always looked so together. I loved her exacting, smart style. There was a freshness to her, an authentic beauty. Not the made-up look—a clear, simple, personal presence. Special.

"You back?" she teased. "I missed you."

I felt as though I had been trapped in some windowless box, unable to communicate. I kept reminding myself, *You are getting better. This is working.*

"Where do you think I was?" I asked.

"I have no idea," she chortled. "You certainly were not in this room."

We laughed, but I knew she was right. A mind is a powerful ally if you need to disappear.

"Someday after you're out of here, I'd like you to teach me that skill," she suggested.

I hesitated. Radcliff made my small life happy, but the idea of her being in it "after I was out" made me uncomfortable. I guess I had not truly entertained the possibility of leaving this room, and now here it was. The look on my startled face was easy for her to read.

"Oh, are you planning to dump me at the hospital exit?" She moved to my bedside and stood over me in her soft, strong way.

She smiled. "That won't be easy." She giggled. "I have plans for us. It doesn't matter how we work it out—I want this person in my life." She picked up the eight-by-ten picture of me Glenna had brought so many months ago, brushing her fingers over the glass.

Our rather heavy discussion ended when we heard a boompa-boompa-BANG! in the hall. In marched my four men in full drag, leading five nursing staff and several patients from my wing of the hospital in a makeshift conga line. As my room filled with people, my body relaxed, my breathing slowed, and my heart filled with love for my wonderful friends. Who would have thought a hospital room could be so full of living, of life, outside of the maternity ward? Not me.

They brought food and champagne, and we all talked and sang and laughed until, out of wonderful exhaustion, I fell asleep. Though my pain was still there, it was less general now, and with some work, I could mostly avoid the sensitive areas. It was like I finally managed to relax. My friends—my family—stayed for a while, their laughter filtering into my welcome state of slumber.

For the first time in a long time, it was a blissful sleep. I dreamed of Hanna and Dr. Sailor having a picnic on the beach. They looked so happy. It was my first sensual dream—I felt like a voyeur. They had great sex, and I think I did, too. *So that part of me is definitely awake*, I thought. It was wonderful news. I wanted to tell Lynna the next morning, but I decided that would be too much information.

She was such a part of my life, but I never wanted to make her uncomfortable with my sexuality. Still, the next time I talked to Dr. Jack Sailor, I couldn't help but smile and think of his prowess back on the sandy beach. His equipment was exceptional, too, at least in my dreams. I couldn't wait to tell Hanna.

We laughed for a long time, and she assured me my dream was correct in that department, though she wouldn't say much else.

She didn't usually talk about their extracurricular activities; her husband, Gary, was my friend, too. Today she told me Jack was an able lover, possibly her best ever. But he also talked with her, listened to her, saw that she was not just "eye candy." She brought him lunch almost every day after mine. His gifts to her were small, thoughtful, and personal. She was in love with him.

As for me, my erotic dreams became frequent and fully enjoyed. I wondered if it was due to the paralysis receding. It seemed strange that I had never had one before the accident, but maybe I didn't need it when I had the real thing. The cast rotated—sometimes Radcliff, sometimes Glenna, sometimes Dr. Sailor.

I was more optimistic now, but not knowing what to expect had become the norm. Losing movement again was still a very real possibility, and it was hard to stay on that midline. One hour it seemed certain I would walk, the next hour, maybe not. People around me wanted to take a careful, middle-of-the-road position. Every one of them pulled toward success, but then caught themselves—careful!

"This was an intelligent gamble," Dr. Sailor cautioned.

"Keep things in perspective," according to Dr. Waters.

"You have more right now than we ever expected a month ago," Lynna reminded. I was feeling jerked around and annoyed. I was also feeling guilty about my attitude every day. It was unsettling to witness myself hanging on every expression. Did they know something? Good or bad? It was hard for all of us. I'm sure they felt me watching, seeking information that didn't exist.

Radcliff was tough enough to listen and understand.

"We all think you're going to get out of that bed," she said. "The only question is when."

Chapter 10
DECEMBER 1963

Physical therapy was now working with me from my bed twice a day. My body would still flame up, but finally after a month, I could actually feel the touch of their hands on my body; not just the fire. Patty, the physical therapist, took a special interest in me. You start to be able to tell. She even took an extra course for new ideas. The careful tracking she offered helped prove the gains I was making.

Every day, we exercised every tiny muscle in my body to combat the atrophy that had taken hold during my months in bed. Push, pull, raise, lower, turn, turn, and start again. We used weights and machines and leg raises to start building a body that could hold my bones up.

Some of the time, I could move my right leg and arm on my own. Well, I think it was me moving things—people near me had learned to duck and dodge my willful body parts. If some poor person got hit, we all rejoiced. It became a silly ritual that signaled progress. I worried I would stay uncontrolled.

The physical therapists had me try to feed myself with little success. But slowly, improvement was happening. I spent more time in a sitting position, and by the end of December, my right side was relatively dependable. The left leg was coming along, but my left arm was still wildly out of sync. Either it didn't move or moved in a creepy, disobedient manner. It always hurt, a strong ache now rather than a burn.

They started asking me to practice making a bridge with my body, with my knees up, feet flat, and butt pushed upward off the bed. I did it on the first try. Someone called Dr. Waters and he brought Sailor.

"We think we can get you on your feet in a few days," Waters said. "We need to talk about traction." That was all I needed to hear—I was getting up!

The next day, Dr. Sailor was there at 7 a.m., with a toolbox filled with pieces of thick metal, plaster, and an array of non-surgical tools. They even smelled like oil, and I couldn't tell if that should be disconcerting.

"You're not going to tie me to the light fixture, are you?" I said, half joking. My eyes were wide with cautious expectation.

"Nope," he answered, suddenly hopping on my bed and positioning his legs on either side of me, straddling my body.

"What the hell?" I exclaimed.

He laughed. "Just keep the faith," he said as Lynna came into the room to assist. She saw my insecure expression and smiled. Her eyes always smiled first, then her mouth.

"Don't worry. I told you—he's a genius." She handed him a thick rectangle of metal, about a half-inch thick, two inches wide, and seven inches long. Then she held up a sloppy pan of plaster. It seemed the plaster went off in every direction. During this time, I had become fastidious about slops and spills on my cast. Though I couldn't see it, I didn't want it to be messy.

After a few minutes of fiddling, they told each other what a fantastic job they had accomplished. Sailor climbed off of me and the bed, and the two of them stood there, big grins on their faces, looking at me.

"What did you do?" I asked.

"We'll wait until the plaster dries. And then," Sailor said softly, "I will cut your traction rope. If all goes well, your cast will hold the traction with a wedge between the tongs in your head and the plaster. And we'll be able to get you up on your feet."

Carefully, slowly, he made sure I understood the last four words: *Up on your feet!*

The news went out to all my friends and the staff. Tomorrow was the day they'd cut the rope. After so many ups and downs, I felt sad, unsure, tearful, maybe depressed. A whole list of what-ifs swirled in my head. *What if this doesn't work? What if this is my only chance?*

In my mind, I kept seeing the doctors' crestfallen faces as I attempted to stand and melted to the floor, a failure.

"Did you sleep?" Lynna said that morning. "The report says you were awake."

"No, I don't think I slept," I groaned. I looked out my window, trying not to cry.

"You're upset, you're frightened—I would

be, too. Just know that this is one try, but they have other ideas," she said. "Don't worry about letting us down, because this is for you. You're so important to us, and we care about you having the life you deserve. Just do what you can, and that's enough." The curve of her soft smile always put me at ease. "It's not your only chance."

Her words were an instant reprieve. It was exactly what had been eating at me. I didn't want to let down the people who were trying to help me. Lynna always seemed to immediately understand, but how, I will never know. Her confidence gave me the courage to try.

A few hours later, Waters and Sailor were there, along with Dr. Vise, Lynna, and a nurse I didn't recognize. The room was filled with electric anticipation as they closed the door.

Sailor took a large pair of ancient, tarnished scissors from the pocket of his smock. "My lucky scissors." He moved out of view behind my head and gently tugged on my cast. "Seems dry and stable," he said.

They all acknowledged his assessment, and before I knew it, SNAP! The rope was cut, and the traction bags made a THUD as they hit the floor. No one said a word. Dr. Waters moved to my bed and pushed the button to raise me to a sitting position, then lowered the bed to the lowest level.

All eyes were on me, and for the first time in several months, I could look straight at their faces rather than the ceiling. They really were grand looking people. They gave me the impression of spectators glued to the final game of the World Series. I was where the action was.

"You're free of that bed," Dr. Waters choked out. He had tears in his bright blue eyes as he took my right hand and held it to his chest. He was trembling slightly. I knew I needed to say something—that this was a big moment.

But I didn't exactly understand why, or what it really meant. I must have looked confused. My mind did not click in. I just sat there.

Lynna came closer. "Tomorrow, we are getting you on your feet," she said. "Tomorrow, you start learning to walk again!"

As I sat at the edge of my bed, it took a few moments to realize I was upright. Everything seemed to be in slow motion. People exited the room one by one, leaving me there on the precipice of the mattress to dangle. I was overcome by a feeling of desertion. Sweat dampened everything inside the cast as I hung onto the circular bed rail, battling a wave of pain, dizziness, and nausea. Why would they just leave me there?

It was as though the pages of a book about the accident, the surgeries, the hospitals, the doctors, the nurses, were being blown by some mysterious wind through my mind. All I could do was watch as they turned. I should be happy. But I was not happy. The emotion coursing through me was more like terror.

It seemed to be true—I was no longer a quad. It felt just as unreal as being told I would never move again. It was like my mind had lost the ability to comprehend anything. Good, bad, yes, no; I couldn't get a clear thought.

My cast felt comfortable and safe. I don't know how long I dangled before I took a chance and tried to move my right leg. Astonishingly, it responded to my signal. I tried to release my grip on the bed rail, and again, it released, just like that. I realized I had never been able to see this room from a sitting position. How long had I been inside these walls?

As I surveyed the large room, I was stunned by the number of intimidating machines crowding the edges. Some I could recognize—oxygen, suction, x-ray—while others were a complete mystery. The walls, to my surprise, were papered in light yellow and green. How had I not known?

A little droplet of sweat dripped off my forehead and into my eye. *Could I walk? Could I stand? Should I try?* Tomorrow seemed an awfully long time to wait after so many months of being stuck. *Go slow*, I thought. *Can I feel the bed under my butt?* Yes, I could.

I was struck again by visions of my limp body melting to the floor the moment I tried to take a step. *But what if I fail?* Then, all at once, it hit me. The lesson Lynna had been trying to teach me during those weeks of fiery pain, at every crossroads where I had nearly given up. Failure wouldn't be found in falling. It would be found in not trying at all.

The bed had been lowered toward the floor, and I could feel the ground under my bare feet, though less so on the left side. Before I could talk myself out of it, I grabbed the bed rail and stood up. I stayed there motionless for a few moments, talking to myself out loud now. "Is this why they left me here?" I asked the empty room. "So I could try?"

Oh my God, I'm standing! This might be my only chance, I thought—so I took it and walked (or more like fell) the short space from my bed to the door, where I held onto the jamb with my right arm and slowly slid down onto the cold tile. I marveled that I could feel the chill of the floor against my skin.

There I was, a crumpled pile on the ground.

But I had walked.

I screamed with joy at the intercom, and soon a gaggle of people appeared to put me back to bed. But I could not be contained. I could walk, or fall, depending how you looked at it, and it did not matter how I might have hurt myself by trying, how I could have ruined the surgery, how I'd acted without consideration. *I can walk*, I thought. *I can walk.* My excitement could not be restrained. The moment my feet hit the floor, I knew I was going to recover.

When the doctors came the next day and asked me to get out of bed, I did. They pulled, pushed, measured, took notes, performed x-rays, and were overall very pleased. I was issued a walker and began to walk and walk and walk.

Any person that came to visit walked with me. The doctors asked that I not go alone, so I always waited for someone to assist me. It seemed most people I encountered in the halls knew I was the Broken Neck. They congratulated me on my good fortune.

The hospital where I'd lived for months but never had the luxury of exploring was set up in a four-sided wing. There was an enclosed courtyard in the middle with a grassy area and a patio with glider furniture. One half of the surrounding square was the ortho wing and the other side was the aged patient ward, mostly elderly women. When I walked through their halls in my head-to-hip cast, with tongs sticking out of my head anchored by two baseball-sized mounds of plaster—inflating my height to about six foot seven—they never seemed to notice. They smiled, said hello, and offered me their hands. There was no fear. Some thought I was their daughter or son. Each time I passed through was like a brand-new encounter for them.

When I encountered regular folks, it was very different. There were always curious adults asking what happened or children running screaming to their parents. I started to stay in my room during evening visiting hours. But that central patio looked so nice, so enticing; I had not been outside in several months. I asked every staff member I saw if I could go out there, but was told no. "Could someone come with me?" I asked. Again, a firm "No!" Even Radcliff, my co-independent, stood firm.

But I could not be deterred. So I slipped out by

myself after lunch one day. It was glorious—even in the slight chill of winter in California, the sun was warm on my pale skin. I drank in the smell of freshly cut grass, the flower-scented real fresh air.

I only took one step on the uneven ground before I lost balance and fell.

Damn, now everyone will be disappointed, was the first thought that sprang to my mind. I was face down on my belly, ashamed to be such an impatient patient. I hadn't even tried to catch myself with my arms to protect my neck, just flopped on my face and cast. I scooted on my stomach across the lawn to a tree and somehow managed to carefully pull myself up.

As I moved toward the patio door, three elderly ladies were sitting on a glider watching me. They just smiled and said hello. I gestured toward myself and laughed softly at the spectacle, but they gave no reaction. I hurriedly slipped back into my room—safe. Exhausted from my self-inflicted fiasco, I conked out.

A few minutes later, a nurse entered the room. She came to the bed and took a good look at me. "Is that a grass stain?" she asked. "It's all around your face opening and your chest," she added, pulling down the sheet. "Did you fall? Were you outside?" I felt like a guilty child.

She called Dr. Sailor. *Oh shit*, I thought. *This is going to be awful.*

I was right.

He came right over, looked at me, and sent me to x-ray. I felt terrible. *Why do I do these things?* I really didn't know. I just needed to go outside! He seemed hurt that I would take such a chance with his neck, his life. *Wait*, I finally thought defiantly. *It's my neck, my life.*

"I don't want to hurt myself," I told him, still feeling childish and stupid. I tried to explain how much I'd needed to be outside, to feel the sun on my skin.

"It seems you do want to hurt yourself!" he almost shouted. I had never seen him get angry. Now his hands were shaking. "This part of your personality, this stubbornness, has worked for you, helped you recover thus far. But now you are taking reckless, ignorant chances. This is not over, Anna. You can still relapse. How can I get it through your head that you're not stable?"

I sought out my ceiling tile and kept my focus there, not speaking or moving.

He paused, his fingers rubbing at his furrowed brow for longer than I liked. His curly hair fell in messy tufts across his forehead.

"A fall could put you back in bed. Your spinal cord is still injured. We don't even know why you're able to walk." He spat as he talked. "Stop acting like a child and listen to us. Please." His posture, usually straight and snappy, was slumped. His smiley face was somber. He still had mustard on his damn tie.

I gave him a solemn look. "Okay, Dr. Sailor. I'll stop celebrating and do exactly as you ask. No more Ice Capades acts. I'm just so relieved to be up." I tried to look contrite. "I do try to be careful, but I know I'm not stable and sometimes fall. I just don't understand why falling outside causes so much more upset than falling here in my room or in the hallway." Was I being defiant again?

He turned and left the room. I didn't sleep that night. I guess fools don't sleep as easy as you'd think.

By the time morning came, the weight of my folly was as clear as the dawning day. This could go wrong. If things went sideways, I would stay there in that bed, just like I'd feared. The fact that I had gotten up could have been the end of me.

This was not over.

The next day, Lynna was back to acting like I was her best patient ever. So, cautiously, I asked her if Dr. Sailor was over his disappointment. She looked cross, but then a small smile appeared on her face.

"Yes, he is," she said. "You have to understand, Anna, your unexpected progress helped all of us, me included. So if you give us a scare, we're going to have a strong reaction. None of us can afford for you to have a major setback." Looking into my eyes, she touched my hand. "We know that on some level it's not fair to you."

She cleared her throat. "I need to know miracles do happen. For myself as well as you. I know you were told I have cancer. I'm looking for that miracle, too." She pressed my hand to her cheek. Her face looked drawn. She really was sick. My stomach clenched at the thought of Lynna in pain, but I was relieved that she wasn't angry. I felt honored to help in some way; to help her hold onto hope.

I thanked Lynna again and again for being honest and confiding in me.

Chapter 11
JANUARY 1964

Once again, my usual day changed. Sam still came, but now we walked. He seemed a little depressed that the See's Candy was no longer available, but without that and with all my walking, he started to slim down. His change was fascinating. His blond, sun-streaked hair began to frame a more chiseled, manly face. My insecure visitor slowly became a confident, rather bold, outspoken man.

Soon he found a boyfriend and started coming less often. Glenna and I missed him but were so thrilled that the time he spent with us helped him in some odd way. He helped me more than he knew every day, simply by being present.

Glenna was still a constant presence. She was always good-natured and very sweet, but something was off. I had a vague feeling that something was shifting between us. Maybe she had found someone else. She seemed to openly sidestep my questions. Radcliff was planning to visit after my release, but there was no date or plan for that yet, so I didn't worry. Hanna still came for lunch; she was still seeing Dr. Sailor. Gary, her George Clooney-look-alike of a husband, visited once a week. Hanna dressed him, so he was always impeccable. I often felt caught in the middle.

Lynna was as perfect as ever, though her illness was starting to show now. We never discussed the cancer again. When I tried, she asked me to ignore that part of her. She said it helped to have important people see the real her without cancer stealing the show. We all die one day, but the thought of Lynna suffering haunted me.

The rambunctious men in my life continued to visit, always offering comic relief. How they came up with the music, the costumes, the shows, I will never know. They were always a hit. The last show they did featured tall, slender Kip dressed as a madam, lanky, red-haired Billy as a working girl, and Mauricio, a beautiful, dark, and mysterious morsel for rent, as the other choice. Kip strutted down the hospital hall like it was a catwalk, dripping in beautiful full drag and holding the leash to a pair of collars around Bill's and Mauricio's necks. It's a wonder we were never arrested. They wrapped colorful streamers around my walker, and we all walked the hallway together, drawing applause from the ladies in the elderly ward and a few tolerant patients. Each drop of joy flowed into the well of my resolve, my will to heal.

As for my condition, it continued to improve, but the bouts of extreme, crippling cramps were awful. If I was in bed, my arms, legs, and head would curl up into deformed, unrecognizable clumps. If I was walking, I could usually get to a sitting position when I could tell it was about to happen. But if I was not seated, I would fall. I was very thankful that I had always been athletic—high dive and volleyball in my younger days—because I know it helped me. Eventually, I got better at falling.

As strange as it seemed, I would sometimes become motion sick, so they supplied me with seasickness pills. Your spinal cord controls so many things.

Despite my progress, I felt insecure about

going home. The place where we'd been living on the oceanfront in Newport Beach was gone, and Glenna had moved home to San Bernardino with her parents. For such a long hospital stay it just made the most sense. Still, it was hard to accept; that house had become a real source of pride for me. But there was no way we could afford to keep it going, and Glenna could stay with her parents rent-free.

We had not discussed finances, and whenever I approached the subject she would say, "We're okay—your job is to recover." I was receiving disability payments that were going into savings, and Glenna said all the bills were taken care of. With no family connection to coordinate with, the hospital had a home transition liaison come visit in early January.

When released, I would go home in my cast for another few months depending on my improvement. The doctors started talking about how to act and take care of myself at home, which mostly involved doing nothing except for reading, eating, and sleeping.

Finally, I realized it was up to me to decide when the transition would happen. With no place to go home to, I was terrified. Just the thought gave me chills. To be honest, I could not even conceptualize what my life would look like after this harrowing experience. I had no desire to return to the rat race I had been running before landing in that hospital bed.

Most of all, I was not ready to give up the support supplied so graciously by the hospital. There were so many wonderful people there who were ready to do anything they could to support my every need and wish.

I still had days where I felt some of the burning pain, and exhaustion would often take over by evening, but overall, at least in my mind, I was on the other side of being a quad. Yes, I was cautioned that it could change—that I was still in the traction and my injury was very present, the spinal cord so cramped for space in my neck. In my mind, it was simple: I thought I could recover and for whatever reason, I was proven right. End of story. As with the other sudden, sad events in my life, I had luck (or maybe an angel) on my side.

My attitude seemed to irritate some around me. They used words like arrogant. But they weren't in that bed; if I was being arrogant, that was okay with me, even if their judgment did leave me feeling depressed at times. So on with physical therapy, and walking, and trying to decide how to restart my life. According to Dr. Waters, I would still have very limited movement. I'd need someone there with me 24/7 at the start. The home transition liaison suggested a nursing home at a very high cost. If I were doing it today, and it was somewhat affordable, that would be my choice. But at that time, it was out of the question.

Mauricio offered to have me move back into the chicken coop, but the boys all had work, and Glenna didn't want to live there. She said she couldn't be there all day—she needed to return to work. *Why now*, I wondered, *after all this time?* I didn't understand why she couldn't stay home for two months or until I could manage.

Then one day, when I went to thumb through a book Glenna had forgotten after her last visit, a handful of envelopes fell from between the pages. They were each stamped with a red-hot warning. PAST DUE.

I could hardly believe my eyes. Things were clearly not fine, as Glenna had so often reassured me.

The next day, I placed the envelopes neatly on my bedside table, ready to greet Glenna the moment she walked through the door. She burst into the room at the usual time, all smiles until her eyes landed on the bundle waiting for her.

"Do you want to tell me what these are?" I

asked, my voice reaching subzero temperatures.

Tears were beginning to prick the corners of her eyes as she shifted nervously on her feet. Cautiously, she took a few steps toward the bed.

"I can explain," she squeaked. Then, like water rushing through a collapsing dam, the words began to tumble out. She told me that she'd been living on my savings so that she could be with me every day at the hospital. By then, she'd also spent the disability payments I'd received so far. My bills had all gone to collections.

I felt like a can of pressurized hair spray on the brink of an explosion as the anger built inside of me. I wanted to scream.

"This is what you've been keeping from me? Glenna, how could you do this?"

Her wrinkled, splotchy face was the definition of an ugly cry, a stream of tears and mucus flooding down her cheeks and nose to drip onto the sterile hospital floor.

"Please," she tried to explain. "I needed to be with you! And everything was so... So discouraging, so hopeless. I just wanted to feel better. I know I shouldn't have spent money on the nights out, the jewelry, but can you blame me? I needed some way to escape, just for a little while!"

She paused, seemingly unsure how to continue.

"And I... I didn't think you'd live through it, at first. I thought if I spent the money, it would only be my problem, not yours."

Suddenly, Glenna was just another part of the bad stuff—all the close calls, the bigots, the mistakes, the infantilization that had made my hospital stay so harrowing at times. Just one more person who had taken the liberty of making my decisions for me. I felt no compassion for her. I never wanted to see her again.

"Just leave," I said quietly, shaking my head as I avoided her eyes.

Glenna's face fell. As she left, she turned back at the door, looking at me hopefully. "I did this for you," she whispered, "so I could be here."

"You did this for yourself," I snarled.

Her calm, sweet voice returned to its normal register. "You'll get over your snit and we'll be okay." She turned and left my room.

The cherry on top was that when they had moved our furniture from the beach to storage, the rental trailer had burst open and our white sofa, chairs, tables, and clothes were dumped onto the Harbor Freeway. Almost everything was lost, and they received a measly fine of $200 for endangering the public. All of this on top of the looming mountain of medical bills and a totaled car, though that part was no surprise. How much would an eight-month hospital stay—plus all the extra care I needed—really cost?

The thought sapped every bit of thankfulness I had cultivated about my recovery.

All of the staff caring for me were concerned about my sadness, but I couldn't tell them what I had learned. Instead, I stayed in my bed, quiet, trying to wrap my head around what my life had become. I was now broke and disabled. I felt unable to think, disgusted by my own "poor me" attitude. I blamed myself for trusting Glenna to the extent that I did.

That evening, Radcliff walked with me on my now-familiar hallway route. She seemed to know not to joke or even talk. As we passed a pay phone in the hall she said, "I'm going to give you my home phone number. Use the pay phone and we can talk." The phone in my room was still not private.

I gladly took the number and one night, after the daily churn of routine had settled, I took my walker out at about 1 a.m. and rolled to the pay phone. I felt I could talk to Radcliff about this but Lynna, it seemed, would have been really angry with Glenna. Rightly so, but... she had enough on her plate. And this was not medical; for once, it was personal.

That night we stayed on the phone for several hours discussing how to handle my situation. The major conclusion was that, after all I had gone through, "This is just about facing the music and working out deals," as Radcliff said. "You have an excellent excuse; you've spent a long period in the hospital. People will help you. I will help you." I believed she was right, and as I listened to her, I began to feel better.

Suddenly, I noticed some people behind me in the dark hall. The pay phone door was ripped open, and two nurses and two attendants grabbed me off my seat. The phone, yanked from my hands, hung off its cord. In my frightened confusion, I wondered, *Would they hurt me*?

"What the hell are you doing?" a red-faced nurse I didn't recognize shouted in my face. My feet hardly touched the floor as all four of them took hold of me. One of the attendants commented on my height, and I tried to mumble something about my walker, to no avail. It clanked to the floor as I reached toward it.

"Let me explain!" I struggled to get free. Their hold was professional and firm, but there was no escape available.

"We thought you'd left the hospital! You can't just leave the ward. You know better than that!"

The nurse's face was contorted in righteous authority as she scolded me, her eyes squinting deep crevices that radiated into her hairline. Her gray hair was pulled back in a tight bun. The others stared at me expectantly.

I tried to say that I didn't know, that I didn't mean any harm, but they had already called the police and my doctors. Finally, I convinced the four of them that I could not sleep and went for my usual stroll with my walker for safety before noticing the phone and calling a friend. After some pleading, they called off the police and the doctors, but they put me on a 72-hour suicide watch.

A security guard was now stationed outside my door at all times.

Lynna's left eye twitched when she was upset. And when she walked in at 7 a.m., it was on high twitch.

"What the hell? You tried to kill yourself?" She threw both arms in the air to exaggerate her disbelief.

"No, Lynna!" I explained what had happened,

and as she listened, her tension began to dissipate.

"Oh, for Christ's sake! You must have really frightened the night crew." She was still exasperated, but a tiny smile crossed her face. "You know, for someone who really tries to follow the rules, you cause some huge fuckups." That sent us both into a fit of laughter.

After we regained our composure, she said, "Let me go take care of this."

Within hours, the guard was allowed to move on.

Chapter 12
FEBRUARY 1964

For some reason, the phone booth incident kicked me out of my doldrums. Radcliff was correct—I could do this. It was just money stuff. My credit and savings would recover eventually. But I still felt uneasy about Glenna. I was angry, mostly with myself for relying on her so readily. I should have had Hanna manage my finances—I'd have probably been ahead on my budget by now. But I never told Hanna what happened.

When I talked with Mauricio about it, he looked me in the eye and said, "Maybe you should consider that she's the one who saved your life. She refused to take you home with a broken neck. Without

Glenna, you'd be dead. There'd be no money, furniture, or credit worries then." He let his words hang in the silent air for a few moments. Then he smiled and softly said, "We've got your back, girl—no worries." He did a dramatic bow and flounced out of the room. I knew he would be there for me, if needed. That was never in question.

But I got the point. He was right. If this ordeal had taught me anything, it was that when your life takes a sharp left turn, the people who come along for the ride are the only thing keeping you on the road. Finally, after about three weeks, Glenna got the courage to call. "Can you forgive me? I love you."

I felt very cold toward her, still betrayed, still angry.

"Of course," I replied. "Please come visit."

If I was to get past this, I needed to talk to her in person.

She was relieved. "I've come up with some answers for us to discuss. Can I come now?"

Within an hour, she was in my room.

As we walked and talked, she told me that her parents, Edith and Hector, wanted me to stay with them until I could be on my own. They said I could stay as long as I needed—no need to pay any rent. They were happy to get Glenna back for a bit and get to know me better. Our dog and two kittens could stay, too.

"What do you think?" Her composure began to slip, tears starting to fall.

I stopped short. "No more bawling, Glenna!" My anger had leaked out. "I want us to get past this, but..."

She cut me off. "I want you to know that I know I acted like a child. I can make this up to you. Please don't leave me. Give me a chance."

"Did you tell them we're in a relationship?" I started walking again. "I don't want to hurt them, lie to them."

"No. I told them you're very important to me and that I had to help you."

"You have certainly done the opposite of that." There it was again—my rage rearing its ugly head.

She stopped in the hall and turned toward me.

"Look, you're not exactly in a position to be prideful. So cut the crap, Anna. They know we have to be in one bedroom. That's as far as I plan to go with my folks. All you need to say is yes or no." She looked me in the eye. "But I won't do this again with you."

She turned and walked back toward my room.

As mad as I was, the intense pressure of going home was beginning to loosen inside me as I thought about living with Glenna's family. She looked up from her book as I reentered the room.

"Yes," I said finally. She nodded and turned

back to the page she was reading.

"Good," she murmured. "Now maybe things will be more normal."

"I hope so," I mumbled back. Then, clearing my throat: "I know how hard this has been for everyone."

"I'll start work for a temp agency tomorrow as a legal assistant. Seems I'm already in demand." Her face lit up in a cautious half smile. "Honey, I want you to know how sorry I am that I messed up so badly. The need to be here with you seemed so important. I thought I was going to lose you." Her voice broke. "I'm sorry."

"We won't speak of it again," I suggested.

And we never did.

On February 25th, I was released to go to San Bernardino. The day before I was to leave, I had the urge to run and hide so I could avoid the goodbyes like I did when I was a kid. It was emotional, saying farewell to the people who had saved me.

Radcliff simply asked that I use her phone number soon and kissed me softly on the lips. It felt dangerous to show affection so openly there, even as I was about to be discharged. But I didn't care. As she left my room, she hovered at the door. "Thank you for all you've done to make my world better, Anna." I felt the tears welling. "I will see you as soon as I can."

Dr. Waters came in shortly after to ask how I was feeling. "Big day for all of us tomorrow."

"Thank you, Doctor. Will you be here in the morning?"

"No, I have surgery." I was sad he would not be part of my last moments in the hospital, but I knew I would see him again soon during the many follow-up appointments that were already on my calendar.

At noon, my special chef came to wish me well and to tell Hanna goodbye, too. We all hugged and cried. "Thank you for all the free lunches," chirped Hanna. She turned to me. "Jack will come in the morning."

The day was like a procession of faces; every person who had come in contact with me in my eight months in that bed. All the aides came by, along with the x-ray technicians, physical therapists—even the tough nurse from the phone booth affair. They all wished me a happy future. It was such a strange cocktail of sadness and exhilaration. I really wanted to go. I really wanted to stay.

My gaggle of gays showed up at 6 p.m., but

there was no show that night. I was too exhausted by my own emotions. By 7:30, I was sleeping.

At 7 a.m. the day I was to leave, I waited to thank Lynna. I wasn't quite sure how to put my gratitude into words, but I needed her to know how much she had meant to me.

But when Dr. Sailor came to give me the final instructions for my transition and confirm my follow-up appointments, he told me that Lynna had asked him to say farewell. She had taken the day off.

"I'm sorry, Anna. She was so attached to you that it was too hard to say goodbye. She asked me to tell you that someday, somewhere, you'll talk again."

I was crushed. How could I leave without saying goodbye? Without knowing for sure that there would be another opportunity to thank her?

"Please, Doctor, can I call her? She's so important. I can't just go and say nothing." He took my hand to console my grief. I was more dependent on Lynna than anyone before or since. As I write this, I still miss her.

"Anna, it's the way it is with patients and caregivers. To the patient, it's personal. But to the caregiver, it's professional. It has to be in order for us to do our jobs. Try to understand." As he reached up to touch my cheek, I saw the mixture of sadness and understanding in his expression. My only response was a choked sob followed by the loud honk of me blowing my nose.

"You'll feel better when your friends come to get you," he said sweetly.

Hanna came in a few moments later. "It's checkout time!" Glenna was next to the bed stuffing things in bags when Mauricio entered.

"I came in with you. It's only fitting we go out together," he said, grinning.

Soon Radcliff was there with the wheelchair, giving special care helping me sit. Glenna gave her the "watch out" look.

"Here, let me push her out."

Radcliff backed away.

The doctor stood up and flashed me the trademark Sailor grin. "Bye for now," he said, touching my cheek again. "I'm so proud of all of us, but you most of all."

In the hall, people waved goodbye. It was a quiet exit.

Then, almost suddenly, we were in the car. It was not an easy task in a cast with an antenna hooked into my head. But we made it.

"I feel sort of in shock," I told Glenna as she promised me everything was ready at her parents' house. As we left the hospital driveway, I startled due to the sharp turn onto the street. "Watch out!"

"Am I going too fast?" Glenna asked.

"A little—thanks," I agreed. I was woozy as I clutched the barf bag they'd supplied me with at the hospital.

"It's an hour drive. We can stop along the way, if you like," she suggested. "It must be such a relief to get out of that room."

I agreed. "But I do feel a little nervous. Exposed, somehow." I stared out of the window, marveling at the trees and the buildings and the people going about their days. Everything that had been just beyond my line of sight for so many months.

"I would love to be in a park before we go home. Is that something we could do? Maybe some terra firma under my feet would ground me." She laughed at the pun.

"Sounds great." Glenna seemed delighted. "There's a park just before we get on the freeway."

It took some care to pop myself out of the car. I will never forget the feeling of stepping onto the soft green grass. The sun warmed my skin as Glenna helped me ease onto the edge of the bubbling fountain at the center of the park. She leaned over and took my shoes off so I could enjoy the cool, rippling water.

Glenna took my hand. "I love you. You can ask for anything you need; I'm here." She scooted closer so our legs were touching, and we just sat there, enjoying each other and the fresh air of the outdoors.

"I didn't think we would ever get here again," she said.

"Yes," I said finally. "I had my doubts, too, but here we are, safe and sound. Well, for the most part, anyway." She giggled through her tears.

"Don't cry, Glenna. We're going to be okay," I said. "Now I feel certain. We'll come out of this stronger and smarter than before."

We drove on to San Bernardino to start our new life.

Chapter 13

Hector, Edith, and Glenna's brother, Ray, were in the yard to greet us with lemonade in hand.

"Come on, have some," Hector offered. "Please feel at home. I have to admit I was surprised by the look of that cast."

I laughed. "Me, too!"

"Come in, I'll get you situated in your room," Edith said.

It was a hard transition, coming home to someone else's house. But they were simple, kind, and generous people, and nothing was asked of me, except that I relax.

"Your job is to get well," Edith said that first day.

My new schedule was wake up, read, lunch at noon—Hector came home to eat with us—then watch As the World Turns, and read some more. Edith took a nap at 3 p.m. Glenna got off work at 5 p.m. and came home to slip seamlessly into the schedule. Dinner was at 6 p.m., then more reading, and bed. I read a book each day, and Glenna kept me supplied. We never mentioned sex. It just didn't seem reasonable at that point, and I didn't have the courage to ask the docs.

On the second night, I figured out I could wash my bottom half with the handheld attachment in the shower. I had only taken sink baths for months, so I was desperate for a proper wash. I waited for Glenna to arrive home. We went into the bathroom, and I carefully stepped into the tub. It was so, so good to feel the warmth of the water and wash my nether regions. But as I stepped out of the tub, with Glenna supervising every move, my tongs suddenly caught on the shower door slider across the top. I had knocked the tongs out of my head!

"You were supposed to watch me!" I screamed at Glenna. She screamed back as she registered the loose tongs. My body went limp, and I slid down the steamy wall to the floor. Edith and Hector came running and joined the screaming.

Finally, we stopped and tried to decide what to do. This was bad. Would I stop breathing?

They all took me to my bed. I was nude from the cast down—we were now better acquainted than any of us wanted. We decided that since we were over an hour from PVH, we should call Dr. Sailor's service. He was out to dinner. "What now?" he answered. When I described the problem, he yelled, "How long have you been home?"

In the background, I heard someone say, "Oh my God," with an Austrian accent. Hanna.

"You can't ride in a car out of traction. Can you breathe?" he said.

Edith gasped. "She can't breathe?"

"No, Mom, she can," Glenna answered.

Hector suggested 911.

"Not yet, Dad, wait and see what the doctor says!"

"Yes, I can breathe. It's fear you hear in my voice," I told Sailor.

"Okay. Put the tongs back in the holes and screw the lever until it's tight."

My heart did a flip. "I can't! Isn't there any other way?"

"You must," he said calmly. The three people in the room stared at me, wide-eyed. My left arm would not go that high, but I grabbed the tongs with my right, found the holes, and fit the tongs into the openings in my skull. I started to turn the screw knob. *Squeak, squeak, squeak.* After a few turns, it was tight, and I could feel the traction again.

"Okay," I said into the phone. "It's done."

My co-panickers loudly sighed in relief. Edith, who had been frozen in place, quietly said, "I'll clean up the bathroom," and left.

"Good. Come to my office first thing tomorrow," Sailor growled. "Stay the fuck out of the shower."

I heard Hanna questioning him in the background. "What did she—" Then Sailor hung up.

I looked at my dismayed remaining housemates and smiled. Hector and Glenna peered back at me, stunned, and turned to leave the room. I stayed put on the bed, feeling like an ass once again.

Early the next day, Sailor was in a better mood. He said I had done a good job; the tongs just needed some adjustments. Again, he asked me to think before I acted. He reminded me that this was not over; it could easily reverse. "Please, be more careful Anna," he pleaded as he stood over me making tweaks. "How many times have I needed to repeat this?"

His chiding immediately put me on the defensive. "I do think before I act. The things everyone seems to focus on are a few mishaps. I live in this cast every moment, and I think I've done the very best

I could to take care." I scowled. "Until you've tried it, don't judge. I don't want to relapse any more than you want me to. I've happily given you the credit for my recovery. Just stop acting as though I want to hurt myself."

Now I was angry. "I don't deserve your attitude. All I wanted was half a shower!"

He was silent for a moment, brow knitted into a cluster of wrinkles. Then his expression softened. "I understand, Anna. You're not wrong." He looked me right in the eye. "But you also have to understand that our pleas for you to be careful are not out of judgment. After everything you've been through, we just want you to be safe." He sighed. "I'll try to trust you a bit more."

I looked around the tidy room, still fuming. Everything smelled like plastic. I desperately wanted out of there. I yearned to have Lynna walk in and say, "She's not a problem patient; give her some credit." Sadly, she did not appear.

"Let's go, Glenna."

Chapter 14
MARCH 1964

After the shower incident, all of my days were alike, but not in the brain-melting way of the hospital monotony. I was very grateful to have such a sweet place to be. It was hot in San Bernardino, even in March, so I mostly had to stay inside. If I overheated in the cast, it took hours to be comfortable again. The fan and a book a day kept me going. After a few weeks, Hanna called for me to come visit in Pomona and I said yes, please! Glenna drove me over to meet her.

At one point, she wanted to vacuum her house, so she put me outside in the early morning cool. The temperature was just right, and I could smell lilacs on the breeze against the backdrop of a bright blue sky. Her recently mowed lawn added to the freshness of the day. I was just sitting under a Chinese elm tree, the weeping branches all around me, when suddenly I felt something tickling my skin under the plaster. I jumped up as I realized there were ants all over me, crawling into my cast. Hanna heard my squeals and came running. After a few minutes of swatting, yelping, and shaking, we managed to remove them all. Hanna felt terrible, but we laughed about it for years to come.

Once, Hanna asked if I had Radcliff's phone number. After I called, Hanna delivered me to her home while Radcliff's husband was away. It was strange, actually, being with one of my nurses. She was a wonderful distraction. Her home was lovely, with clean, Asian-inspired design. That décor choice had surprised me. But I came to realize it was like a reflection of her—beautiful, simple, elegant. There was a large living room filled with plants and candles, and the bedroom was dressed in a brown, beige, and black color scheme punctuated by a round king-sized bed. That was not common in 1964. I was very impressed.

"Are you comfortable?" Radcliff asked, sitting down close to me on the couch.

I shifted my body away slightly. Before, I had

always been safely distanced in my large hospital bed. This was a different dynamic, and my mind needed to catch up.

"You must need space," she wondered aloud. "I'll get us a drink." As I watched her go toward the kitchen, she suddenly turned. "Caught you looking." She grinned. I felt my face turn red. "I'm glad I can still catch your eye. I thought I might need my uniform."

"You always surprise me, Radcliff." She came back into the room holding two glasses of water. "You quit drinking?"

"Yes," she said. I blinked back at her, not quite sure what to say.

"Why would you want to be with a person in a cast?" I asked.

"Because I love you," she answered, almost casually. "And if we're going to be in a relationship, I need and want to be present and sober." A hint of concern snuck into her expression, but within a few seconds she was back to Nurse Neutral.

I was shocked. "But you don't really know me. How can you be so sure?"

"Working as a nurse you learn about people as they are, not what they look like or project themselves to be. And you did bring that picture for me, remember?" she said.

My face was hot again. "I didn't realize you knew that photo was for you."

"I've known you for several months now. I do know what and who you are." She swirled the water in her glass. Maybe it was a reflex; the muscle memory of being a former drinker. "Watching you go through this recovery was hard for all your caregivers. But I learned you are trusting as well as trustworthy. You are honest. And you are true to yourself—nonmonogamous, even under pressure to change."

I was touched by her sincerity, but it also scared me. She went on to tell me that many of the things that had gone wrong in her life had gone wrong because she drank too much. She'd almost been fired when she was accused of using my drugs. I heard Dr. Sailor's words in my head: *Stop taking chances.* But I pushed the thought away and took her hand.

"Let's go to bed," I said. It was my first try at being sexual since the accident, and I didn't care that I hadn't cleared it with the doctors yet. I felt safe with this woman, albeit unsure of how this would work out in a head-to-butt cast. But she never hesitated, and we fell into a rhythm of slow, easy loving. It was one of the best intimate experiences of my life, and my first as a "walking quad."

At about 3 a.m., still awake, I felt my sixth sense kick in. Someone was outside the window. I had to sort of throw myself up to stand due to the cast, then went to the end of the bed. I was right; someone was standing there.

I took hold of the venetian blind string and pulled it up fast. On the other side was a very surprised Black man. We did that startle dance, him jumping first and then me. His eyes opened wide when he saw me. I just stared at him, never feeling frightened. My sex-soaked mind tried to react. "Is Vonetta here?" he squeaked out.

"No, she's not," I answered. He turned and walked away, then stopped at her sidewalk to look at me again in stark disbelief before striding off.

She was up on one elbow looking a combination of embarrassed and surprised. I smiled. "I don't need to be your only. It's no problem."

She hesitated. "Okay."

I jumped, as best I could, back into bed. She was as appealing out of her clothes as she was in them. Perhaps even more.

We spent several more weekends together at her house, but as time passed, she became impatient. After all her talk of relationships, I decided seeing each other hurt more than it helped. So I just didn't go again. I always intended to get in touch once I could drive, but I never did.

My time with her helped me through some of my worst moments, and I still think of her with great respect and affection. Mauricio saw her one night at a party a few years later. He said he was drunk, sitting on the floor, and she was just as drunk as he was. She recognized him from the hospital, but she did not ask about me. They just sat there, extremely intoxicated, holding on to each other and weeping. He said it was a soggy but sweet reunion.

When he told me, I had to excuse myself from the table to go to the bathroom and weep.

I loved her dearly, but I did not try to contact her again.

In April, I had the appointment with Dr. Sailor to take my cast off. My traction had been removed two weeks before. The cast was a part of me now, and it took all of my courage to walk into his office that day. This seemed my last step out of this nearly yearlong detour in my life.

All the plans I had made no longer seemed important. I'd lost interest in running the practice

I'd been preparing to build in La Jolla before my accident. The state rehab offered to pay for more education, but I couldn't think of anything I wanted less. Someday, some way, I would use my degree. But I had no desire to spend my second chance at life chasing after some mirage of "success." For now, all I wanted was freedom, not to be tied down by others' needs. I had enough needs of my own.

Sailor took one look at me and saw my hesitation. "Feeling insecure after living in this state for so long is normal. You're correct in your assumption that you'll feel very upset for a few days." He grinned. "You will experience some motion sickness again—don't ask me why, it just happens." I said nothing. He cleared his throat. "I wish you could just step out of that cast and walk away like nothing happened. But you've been on a life-changing journey, and it's not over yet. You must be careful and very patient with yourself."

By now, I had learned to listen and follow his instructions. He reminded me that he could prescribe medication if needed for my anxiety.

His office nurse set me up in a room that resembled a cast lab, with plaster molds of all shapes and sizes hanging from the walls. She chattered on as I waited for the doctor to come back. "I hope you know you're the doctor's favorite patient. He says you're smart, reasonable, never gave him a problem." After all of my mishaps since regaining my mobility, it was so special to hear that I wept. I knew that I had in fact given him problems with my brazenness, but I appreciated his restraint not to say so. *Specialist doctors are an odd group*, I thought to myself. *What you see is never what you get.*

"I didn't intend to make you cry, sweetheart!" Sailor's nurse stammered.

I put my hand up to assure her I was okay. Her kind expression and nurse's smile told me she understood.

"It's okay, she deserves a few tears. She's been so stoic," Dr. Sailor said as he walked into the lab. "Let's get this done." He rubbed his hands together in anticipation.

He put me on a stool again—no rollers this time. As I looked at them, all I could think of was how much I missed Lynna. I secretly hoped she might be there. She had been by my side for both castings, so I thought seeing it removed might be enticing enough to draw her out. Until now, she had always managed to be in the room for all of this. But she was nowhere to be seen.

There were many times I thought I would never be sitting on that stool. Everything I'd been through was flashing through my mind like a procession of images clicking through a slide projector.

"Boy, it's been a long road to get to this day. So many people helping me. It has been an incredible journey. It's taught me so many lessons." I looked up at Sailor hopefully. "Do you ever see Lynna?" He ignored my question.

"It has been a long road," Sailor said, "and this is better than any of us had dared to hope for. But don't forget, Anna, it's not over. You'll be in a four-post brace for several months. Things can still go wrong."

I groaned. *Always with the caution*, I thought.

I looked at this wonderful man, with his sparkling, dark brown eyes, his contagious, toothy grin and his Tony Curtis curly hair. I think there was an unidentifiable brownish stain on his lab coat. To this day, my respect for him has never dimmed. Though I appreciated Dr. Waters just as much, I felt closer to Sailor somehow. It might be that the Hanna factor tinged my perceptions.

The saw—the one that would not cut skin—was deafening inside the cast. One long cut to my underarm, one around my neck. God, it was noisy. The last cut went straight up the back to the top of my head. He was handed a pry tool, and with a great creaking sound, I was out and free—and freaked out.

It must be how a baby bird feels exiting its shell. When Sailor touched my shoulder, I jumped. I was not used to the skin-to-skin contact. He looked concerned then laughed. "You felt that—that's great!" The nurse lathered me up, wiped me down. The scent of soap cleared the damp, dirty cast odor.

"I want that cast," I told them, almost frantic. "Don't throw it out." They reluctantly wrapped it for me in a large trash bag, like the world's most macabre take-out container.

I had lost so much weight during my months in the hospital that I could hardly recognize my body. At six feet tall, I was only about 120 pounds. It was shocking! They helped me put on a bright orange sweatshirt and stood me up. The cast alone weighed about 20 pounds, so to say I felt light on my feet was an understatement.

"You will need to learn to walk again, but it won't take as long as when you first stood up. Your balance will correct quickly," assured Dr. Sailor. "Also, your skin will start to peel and renew itself. Try to stay out of the sun."

They guided me to the waiting room until I was stable, and Glenna and Mauricio helped me to the car, one on each side. Finally, I was a free woman.

Mauricio owned a salon, and I needed my hair (what was left of it) washed and trimmed. At that point, I was almost bald with several long, stringy pieces that had been missed at the recasting shaved head event. It was a stunning look, I must say.

At the salon, they treated me like I was very breakable. At one point, I turned my head for the first time in several months, and my body instantly turned into a noodle. I collapsed right to the floor. We all were terrified, but I was right back on my feet in moments. Then, after he sat me in a chair and covered me with a plastic salon drape, the chair somehow broke and fell backward. Luckily, Mauricio caught it, and disaster was averted. I still can't believe that happened. Suddenly feeling overwhelmed, I started to wrinkle up for the ugly cry.

We were all so frightened that someone started to giggle, and then we couldn't stop. It was, as I remember, the best laugh I'd had since this all started. Throughout this whole mess, laughter had been one of my best remedies. It never failed to break the tension of moments that threatened to crack me open.

Finally, they put me in the car, and we headed for San Bernardino, and Glenna's parents' home, and bed. The brace was very uncomfortable. I was so accustomed to that cast.

Everything hurt; I took some pain pills, and it was lights out.

I woke up the next morning, still hurting all over, but so excited to have progressed to this point. For the last few months, I'd had to compensate for the cast, so without a thought, I pulled my knees up and threw my body out of bed as I had done for so long. This time, without the extra weight of the cast, I catapulted my body straight into the open bedroom closet.

Oh no, I thought. *Not again!* It was still early dawn, not quite light yet. Maybe I could get up on my own, and no one would know. But no.

It made so much noise, everyone in the house was there within minutes in various states of nudity. Glenna, Edith, Hector, and even Glenna's brother, Ray, plus our two kittens and our dog, Linko, had gathered to peer into the closet. I had dived headfirst into a shoe rack, my bare butt sticking up to be viewed by all.

As they all ran into the room, I grew more embarrassed with each arrival.

"Are you okay?" Hector finally asked. He was always sympathetic and concerned, perhaps the most nonjudgmental person I had ever met.

"How would I know?" I answered, my voice muffled by a boot. They got me upright and back on the bed. We laughed big snorting laughs. Edith ran off to pee, and the men realized they were without pants and scurried away. I lay there looking at the smooth plaster ceiling. Glenna realized how silly I felt and tried not to laugh anymore, but she soon lost that battle. The bed shook with our uproarious, thankful laughter. She deserved the release, even at my bruised ego's expense.

This is not over, I thought. *Maybe it will never really be over*. But I had stopped caring by that point, I realized. I was starting to feel indestructible. *Come on, life. I'm ready.*

But there was one area where I certainly did not feel invincible. Our financial situation was dire. Glenna had still not contacted anyone about our bills, most of which were in my name and in collections, and the hospital tab had not arrived yet. It was so depressing, on top of the depression that seemed to be a natural part of my injuries. Face to face with no permanent place to live, no job, no savings, and no credit, I panicked every time I tried to think it through.

Edith was such a sweet, simple woman (in the best possible way). She kept telling me, "You're twenty five years old. You'll be okay. Just give yourself a chance to completely recover." After a while, I recognized that was my only choice.

And somehow, it worked.

198

Chapter 15
MAY 1964

A few weeks later, the dreaded hospital bill arrived. We all sat quietly at the kitchen table to open it. I was ashamed that my hands were shaking. My mind was racing. *How will I ever pay this?* I took the envelope in my hands and opened it at the top with a paring knife. It was a threefold letter.

When I began to scan the words, I could hardly believe my eyes.

"The hospital, your two doctors, and your staff have contributed to your stay. Your part, other than your miraculous recovery, is $1,000. Stay well, stay positive. You taught all of us something with your undying will and strong recovery."

All I could do was stare at the letter. No words came to me as chills ran up and over my body. Glenna took the paper from my hand and passed it over to her parents. None of us spoke. In time, I left to go into the bedroom. There was no way to express my shocked gratitude.

Glenna came in and sat next to me on the bed, but she didn't break the silence. This had given me a chance—a new start at life. Thanks to this massive gesture of support and generosity, I was not buried in hospital debt for years. I was free again. I was *well* and free. I took this as absolute proof—I truly was a protected child of God.

I could walk, think, pay my way. It was as though I saw the sun at dawn.

Within about three months of my release from the hospital, we asked Mauricio if we could move back into his backyard chicken coop apartment. Glenna was working, and I could drive again. Even the four-post brace didn't last very long. I did wear it until I got a job, and the doctors asked that I keep it on after that, but I just couldn't. No hair was enough of a concern when it came to interviews; the metal brace had to go!

My pain increased slightly without it, but after so many months confined to my plaster cast, it was like my body rejected any attempt at constraint. Even when I tried sleeping in it, I would wake up to find it tossed across the room.

My job search had been more fruitful than I expected. G. David Schine of the Los Angeles Ambassador Hotel bought a property in Pomona, and I was hired there as a sales manager. Two weeks later, I was made resident manager. It was not a popular Pomona fixture at the time—originally named the Brizilla, it was known as a brothel in a town with the most churches per capita in California.

We had a mauve dining room that seated 80, a pink coffee shop, a lobby with a two-story waterfall, and the largest ballroom in the area with capacity for 300. We offered 200 rooms, all facing a large, beautiful pool, as well as a nice bar spacious enough for live music. My favorite part was choosing the performers for the live acts, but they also seemed happy with how I handled the staff and the guests.

I was so excited to have work, and it would become my favorite job, even to this day. The owners changed the name to the Pomona Valley Inn, toned everything down to beige, brown, and a touch of orange—'60s chic—and began offering a free carafe of wine with dinner. Long story short, within six months we found an excellent team and percentages went from 8% to 120%. I spent most of my time at work. Hanna visited frequently, along with my Pomona men, though as the buttoned-up version of themselves. Being noticeably gay would not fly at that hotel.

Even so, I loved it. It was like having a huge house and my job was simply to entertain.

JUNE 1964

One evening, my boss, Mr. Schine, landed on our helicopter port in the back lot to reward my hard work with a $3,000 bonus check. That was a lot of money in the '60s. That very welcome check afforded me a car, took care of my hospital bill, and paid off all of my standing debt. Now I was a much more experienced human due to the accident, but I felt I was taking my position at the starting line again. There was no way to explain the depth of my gratitude.

That night on the way home, I drove to a nearby park that I liked. I sat there looking out over a lush green hillside, trying to wrap my mind around all that had happened. The fear and pain of those awful months in the hospital were now diminished. The love, compassion, and support were what I remembered.

All I was trying to do on July 12th was get home from a night out. Then the accident happened, and my life changed forever. The people that pulled me through came into my life, helped me survive, and then left again. I missed them so much, but they were gone. Sometimes I almost wondered if it had all been a mirage.

The moon was coming up, and I realized I was late getting home, but as I started the car, with every bit of my mind and body working, I paused and turned back to my uncompleted life again. I had no doubt that I was the most fortunate of all women.

As I drove past the picnic area, I stopped. Having been there many times, it was so familiar and yet foreign. The clouds, full moon, and intermittent rain were taking turns dancing with the green, grassy slope. I stepped out of the car to stand in the soft, misty rainfall. The urge to feel it on my skin took over and, almost without thinking, I removed my clothes. No one else was there, but I'm not sure I would have cared.

I walked the 20 feet to the soft grassy area and lay down. As I lay there feeling the wet lawn, the damp, cool breeze, the rain on my body, I thought about feeling nothing for so long. Even now, a rainy day is the feeling of total comfort to me. When I was still living with Hector and Edith, Glenna and I used to sneak behind the garage to perform our own private rain dance. The moisture on my skin was always like a message from above: I was alive.

As the rain began to soak me down to my bones, I thought about Lynna, so consistent, so strong, willing to help in any way. One tear slid down my cheek, seamlessly fading into the rain. She was really gone. The clouds parted, and moonlight lit the area, then disappeared again. That's what Lynna had been like. A beam of moonlight in the darkest stretch of my life.

I thought about Sam, who came every day and just sat with me, supporting as best he could. Hanna, my daily lunch date, who was right there when I needed a loving friend for my recovery at home. My Pomona boys, who never failed to make me smile. My doctors, who took chances on my behalf. Glenna and her family, who helped me without expecting anything in return. And Vonetta, who accepted me as I was, even knowing on some level that one day she would not be in my life.

The ability to feel, think, and recover was never promised, but here I was, in my birthday suit—intact. In that moment, I promised myself I would use my life for something good, or at least never for bad. I slowly walked to the car, my feet wanting to cling to the grassy earth, and got dressed in my now-wet clothes. Then I drove out of Genisha Park and never returned.

Later, I would see the sign and think of it as a sacred place. That place was an ending—a place to leave the bad times and pick up living.

That sweet, stormy night, I left the fear, loneliness, and paralysis in the park and entered my new life.

I would soon be 26 years old.

Epilogue
JUNE 2017

I shuffled into the coolness of the garage, reaching up to tug on the pull cord attached to the solitary light bulb that hung from the ceiling.

My eyes swept over shelves of boxes and miscellaneous objects as the space was flooded with artificial light. This house in Santa Barbara was full of memories—a whole life's worth of moments lived on borrowed time.

A few weeks prior, for the second time in my life, I had been told that my days on this earth were numbered. I'd suffered a heart attack (not my first) and, though the doctors had inserted a stent, they weren't optimistic that I'd last beyond Christmas.

It was time to get my affairs in order.

I didn't want my loved ones, and especially not the seven children I'd raised as my own when a relative could not, to be stuck with the job of tossing out my junk. So here I was, preparing to sift through the collection of items that summed up my small, happy existence.

As I stood there, my gaze was drawn to a spot high on a shelf, tucked away in the back corner. The yellowed plaster was wrapped in a sheath of plastic coated in a thin layer of dust. It had been months, if not years, since I'd pulled out my old cast. I reached up to free it from its hiding place.

Most people who got a look at it would wrinkle their noses in disgust, either at the faint smell that still lingered around it or at the mangled edges of the stained plaster. "Why on earth would you keep that thing?" they'd say.

The truth was, holding on to it never felt like a choice. It had become an extension of me, as integral as an arm or a leg. It was the most expensive thing—emotionally, physically, and financially—that I ever purchased. It was also possibly the most worthwhile investment I ever made.

The woman who went into that cast was not the same woman who came out of it. I had emerged changed; transformed.

Until the Broken Neck forced me to slow down, I'd never stood still long enough to realize what I was missing. I was always rushing, putting one foot in front of the other in the race to enact my grand plans. My laser focus on success had blinded me to the more human values of life. But once I was in the cast, those human values, those relationships, were all I had left. Suddenly, it seemed nothing in the world could be more important.

It felt like an honor—a privilege—to learn that lesson at only 24 years old.

As the years went by, my mind held fast to the memory of how it felt to have a tiny assist when, for the first time in my life, I could not achieve what I needed on my own, no matter how simple the task. I had been saved by the kindness of strangers and the strength of my own resolve, and I promised myself I would always look for chances to carry that good will forward.

It colored every decision I made from the day I was released. It propelled me to abandon my pursuit of clinical psychology and instead open a vocational school, where I could help all kinds of young people and offer my counseling for free to those who could not afford it. I spent two decades there, supporting young girls just starting out and college students struggling with difficult situations at home. In some ways, it was like showing up for a younger version of myself who'd desperately needed someone in her corner.

Even in retirement, it motivated me to offer a hand up to anyone who came to me in need, no matter their circumstances. I knew from my time in the CircOlectric bed that even when it seems all hope is lost, there is always another idea, another method, another person who can spark it again if you just keep looking. And if I could light that fire for just one life on the brink of giving up, it would all have been worth it.

Standing here now, on the precipice of my second date with death, I still didn't want to part with the cast and all it symbolized. Yet some piece of me knew that it was time—that it had to be me, not my friends or my family, who would turn the page on this chapter of my story.

I took a deep breath, feeling the chalky texture of the plaster between my fingers, and silently thanked the cast for the lessons it had taught me. Then I rewrapped it in plastic, placed the bundle on the trash pile, and went back to tidying up the remains of my long, happy, hopefully meaningful life.

Little did I know that Christmas would come and go, and I would keep on living.

And I still haven't stopped.